THE
FORGOTTEN
SOLDIER

THE FORGOTTEN SOLDIER

MORTARMAN

To John

From Carroll Durham

8-6-14

CARROLL DURHAM

To order additional copies of this book, contact:
Xlibris Corporation
1-888-795-4274
www.Xlibris.com
Orders@Xlibris.com
81438

CONTENTS

Picture of me graduating from high school

Photo of me before I went to Vietnam

PREFACE

To be a good soldier is no easy feat. It takes fortitude, determination, and faith along with tenacity to complete the mission. I am an African American patriot of the 1960s. I was diagnosed with post-traumatic stress disorder in 1993. While in Vietnam, I received no Purple Heart. The medals I did receive were three bronze stars along with thirteen other medals for heroism, which included two commendation medals with the oak-leaf clusters.

My journey as an African American soldier at the young age of nineteen was preceded by relatives who made sacrifices for me. These relatives were soldiers in the Civil War, World War II, Korean War, and the Vietnam War. Through the countless hours of rehabilitation with the veterans administration, my story was formed to show how I went through the onset of post-traumatic stress disorder.

This is a story about black youth during the civil rights movement in the United States. As a young boy in Washington DC, there was a feeling of being a warrior. In 1959 at the beginning of the Vietnam War or when the Vietnam War started, there was a fresh sense of victory after World War II. To be a soldier during this period was something to be admired. To come from a military family, it was felt like a time for adventure.

At the same time, when I became nineteen years old in 1968, after graduating from high school, there was a sense of knowing that I would be called upon to do military service for my country. My decision was made to become a voluntary draft for two years in the army. My preparation for being a warrior in Vietnam had been set in motion. To overcome fear was paramount while I was in the battlefield of Vietnam.

To be confronted and intimidated by millions of enemy soldiers, along with thirty thousand American soldiers who got killed in 1968 and 1969, meant that I was not to come back alive. I fought along with several nationalities from all over the world that were integrated into the combat units in Vietnam. President Harry Truman issued a message to Congress stating all segregation in the U.S. military would end in 1948, when I was born.

ACKNOWLEDGEMENTS

Due to the amount of time and energy that I have committed to this book, I will not be able to recognize all contributors who helped me along the way. I will be able to give you some names of the people that influenced me the most through this journey. They will be people from various walks of life. First of all, I would like to thank God. I would like to thank Carroll A. Durham Sr., for the service to his country. I would also like to thank my mother, who was associated with the military along with other family members. Last but not least, my acknowledgement to my wife, Cynthia, for enduring the life of a writer. I also want to thank my college bound son and daughter, Troy and Monica for being a part of this journey with me.

The education influence will not go without recognition. I would like to thank all of my elementary school teachers from Washington D. C. during the nineteen fifties. The Bainbridge Naval Training Station in Maryland, also contributed to my education at this time. The other schools that attributed to my education are Stone Hill middle and Bates middle school in Sumter South Carolina, along with the defunct St. Jude High School—also in South Carolina where I graduated. My education in military training continued on boot hill at Fort Jackson in South Carolina in nineteen sixty eight, along with my additional advanced infantry training until my departure to Vietnam. Thanks to my military comrades in the second and fifth infantry reconnaissance unit connected to the First Calvary division, where I continued my learning curve during my one year deployment in Vietnam as a mortarman squad leader in nineteen sixty eight and nineteen sixty nine.

Last but not least, I would like to recognize the Historical Black College, Barber Scotia College, where Mary McCloud Bethune attended. I received my bachelor of arts degree in Sociology in nineteen seventy five under the GI bill. I would like to thank past, President Mabel McCain, while I attended the college located in Concord, N. C. Thanks to my college associates who continue to encourage me. They are Fellowman Raymond Clark, Nathaniel Monroe, Barry Hampton, Nathaniel Parham, John Conquest, Glen Brown, James Hill, Charlie Johnson, David Nesbit, Harry Payne, Barry Sims, Robert Simpson, and Woodrow Williams. Best regards go out to attorney and fellowman, Larry Newell, who also helped in the process. Thanks to the mentors that helped me through this process. They are Clarence Davis and Max Friedlander who spent countless hours with me on this endeavor. The participation of the Veterans Administration cannot go without notice. Thanks to

Gerald, from Federal Express in Baltimore, along with David who helped me with photos, which also includes photographer James Lewis. Thanks also go to Mary Lou and John Coyle of Coyle Studio in Towson Maryland. I would also like to thank the staff of Xlibris for their interest in my project.

CHAPTER 1

NORTH AND SOUTH

It was a star-filled night on the Fourth of July in Washington DC. The sky was full of fireworks. I crawled up to the window that was in a dark room upstairs. I got up under the window curtain so I could get a good view. The fireworks seemed as if they came right at me. I was protected by the window as I looked down toward the street and saw people who lit the fireworks from the ground. They seemed to be in precision. Little boys and girls ran around excited. They jumped up and down in excitement. Another fireworks display came past the window.

People rode by in cars and honked their horns. People hung out car windows and waved American flags. A white boy jumped out of a car that stopped. He bent down and pulled some firecrackers out of his pocket. He put the firecrackers on the ground and lit them.

The firecrackers soon went off as he jumped back to his surprise. The firecrackers exploded in different directions as the boy fell back. He soon got back in the car and yelled out the window, "Happy Fourth of July!" The car screeched and sped off.

It was in the early fall of 1952; with pinned white diapers on, I crawled around in an almost empty living room in a public housing project on 5747 East Capitol Street, Washington DC. I crawled from corner to corner, expecting to find something to get into. My bright brown eyes were sharp and visual. My curiosity took me to several corners of the house. I sat up and gazed in a corner. I was now spellbound and fixated on a new discovery. The items were an army helmet, an ammunition box, web gear, with bullets and a .45 holstered in a black leather case. I crawled toward the armaments. They were something for me to have. I wanted to be my own man boy and become a pretend soldier as I put the helmet on my head.

As a country boy in South Carolina, the desire to be a soldier was there. It was good for me to crawl and see the things that were around me. Everyone seemed like they enjoyed being around me. Somebody would always pick me up. I could remember one of my aunts saying, "Oh, what a fine boy this is. He's so cute. One of these days, I'm going to take you home with me." I just wanted some time to myself even though I was a small boy. Being picked up had become less fun for me.

One afternoon, my parents wanted to visit some of my relatives nearby in South Carolina. They lived a few miles up the road. There was a wooden crib in the kitchen that I played in. The play crib was right in the kitchen where we would eat. I could see my mother and dad's bedroom right across the kitchen. There were only two rooms in the whole house. The kitchen table was right in front of me. The table was wood on top, with metal legs and four metal chairs with plastic on them. Right in front of the table was a cupboard and an iron stove. Pots hung up on the wall in the left corner.

Further to the left was a big fireplace. The heat from the coals glowed red from a fresh batch. The crackle of the fire woke me up. I took a look around the cabin. There were a few lanterns that hung on the beams in the room. My mother and father talked in the next room while I listened with intent. I looked over to the other side of the crib and saw a little teddy bear. One of his eyes was gone, and a half of an ear was cut off. I ran and jumped on the teddy bear without hesitation as I grabbed the bear and shook it with all my might.

Without a stitch of clothes on me, I pushed the door further open to the small-framed house. The road was red dirt that turned dusty when it was dry outside. Along the edge of the road were ditches, where the peach orchards spread out beyond the road. On the road in front me, I saw an old black man, with an old green army coat and a worn calvary hat on tilted down in front of his eyes, who steered a mule. The old man was slumped over as he held the reins in his hands while the mule moved slowly up the road.

As I crawled out further into the road, a bull roamed free in the meadows. It soon came up on the road and spotted me. It snorted and patted its feet on the ground as it started to make its charge toward me. There was a well on the other side of the road that caught my eyes. The bull started its run toward me. My dad yelled my name. He said, "Junior! Junior! Junior!" He pulled the door open further and saw what was about to happen. He ran toward me with a burst of speed.

He scooped me up and ran toward the well. It wasn't long before he had me in his arms on top of the well. The old man in the wagon heard the commotion and turned the wagon around, with the mule picking up speed as he got closer to the bull. The old man jumped off the wagon and got in front of the bull as it circled the well. He had a big stick in his hand to distract the bull, which it did as the bull turned around and went in the opposite direction. My dad jumped off the well along with me and thanked the old soldier who felt he had done his duty.

The city of Washington DC was where my dad wanted to find some work. Work was hard to find for a black man. My dad struggled to find work that was suited for him. I would have to get used to city life. My mother would find a job right away. She would work as a secretary for Andrews Air Force Base. She would get the job quickly because she had a college degree in business administration.

I started to notice pictures of war more and more on television in the early 1950s. The horses the cavalry men rode in the military impressed me as I watched them tame the West. Their ability to escape from their enemy intrigued me. I would soon face my first form of physical hostility.

My dad held on to my hand as we walked out of the door of the apartment. I was surprised when a mud pie smashed against my face. It was thrown by a little black boy who played in the mud next door. My reaction was astonishment as I brushed the mud off my face. My father then said, "Don't let that boy hit you like that." In an instant I knew I had to defend myself. It was not long before a mud pie was slammed into the face of the boy. The mud pie thrown by me caught the little boy off guard. The boy lunged at me. My dad bent down and balled up my fist for me and put me in a boxer's stance. All of a sudden the encounter got more intense as I and the boy struggled in our awkward manner. We began to tussle and get a few blows in. My father said "Don't you let anyone take advantage of you," as he pulled me off the boy.

I soon met a black boy named Red. He had red hair and was about my age. We played with our toy soldiers and set them up in different positions for defense and offense. We divided the soldiers up between the little hills where we played at.

We were being watched by members of the neighborhood gang. They did not like us to be together. We had also been asked to join their gang by the gang leader, whose name was Buster. Buster looked rough and was a streetwise kid. He was kind of short and stocky, just a couple of inches shorter than I was.

One day, Buster saw me and Red while we played with our toy soldiers. Buster decided to intimidate us by charging up and down the hill where I and Red played. There were about ten or eleven boys in the group carrying sharp sticks who tried to look like African warriors; they also had dogs with ropes around their necks, but that didn't bother me and Red because we felt that as long as Buster and his gang didn't interfere with our toy soldiers, a fight could be avoided.

As I sat between two project buildings on a mound of dirt with my soldiers, I looked around, and Buster was storming toward me in a rampage with his gang members. Around the corner, there was a tree about a hundred yards away near a fenced yard. Before I realized it, the dogs were on my heels as I jumped on the fence and started to climb the tree. I looked down at the angry gang as they cursed me, along with the dogs who barked with excitement. Buster looked up at me and sneered. The next thing I heard was my mother calling me. The gang soon departed. My mother looked up at the tree and said, "Junior, get down from that tree so we can eat dinner." I started to gain a little confidence in myself as I grew bigger.

One day, my mother told me to go to the store so that I could get some bread. This was the first time I would cross the street to get something for my mother. There was a Japanese family that owned a store across the street. This was on Independence Avenue in Washington DC. We lived in the basement of a tenement house. I would see the Japanese people go in and out of the store from time to time. They looked unusual to me because of their slanted eyes.

My mother said, "I want you to go to the store, here is some money." We stepped out in the small front yard. My mother gave me a nudge. "I want you to go to the store across the street and get some bread. We need some bread for dinner. I want you to watch the cars before you cross the street. I want you to look both ways." As soon as I stepped off the curb, a yellow convertible speeded toward me. It was going at a high rate of speed. As soon as the driver saw me step out into the street, he hit his brakes.

The car came to a screeching halt. I was astonished and frightened at the same time. The convertible almost hit me. My mother ran to me and grabbed me. I shivered in her arms. She said, "Son, are you all right?"

As I searched through my father's dresser, I came across a box of bullets. My fascination made me want to do something with my discovery. There was only about twenty-five yards between my house and the next-door neighbor's house, which was made of brick. All the projects looked alike in Washington DC. I sneaked the bullets out of the house along with my father's gun belt without my parents knowing it. There was a mound between the two houses so that I could duck when I threw the bullets up against the wall. I positioned myself as if I were in combat.

I got a bullet out of my pocket and reared back to throw it like a baseball against the wall. The bullet hit the wall and sounded like a small firecracker that had gone off as I ducked. A few of the bullets

I threw would not make this sound. When I went to inspect what had happened, some of the bullets would have blunted heads.

I watched the American soldiers fight the Japanese soldiers on television with intensity.

The great battles, skirmishes, and massacres or standoffs intrigued me as I continued to watch their acts.

I was all excited the day before school because I had been psyched up for the big event of my life. The first school day arrived. I woke up early that morning to get prepared for school. My skin shined from the vaseline that was put on my face. Being small in stature would make you think I wasn't recognizable in a crowd. It was also an asset. I was able to blend into the crowd as a way of not being seen.

Students passed by me as I stood in the hall of the elementary school. An envelope was in my hand. My eyes were closed when I ripped open the envelope. The card was folded back in my hand. None of my classes had a passing grade on it. I had failed the third grade. Emptiness came inside of me. A student passed by me and snatched the report card out of my hand. He looked at the card and started to laugh. He said, "I can't believe you failed third grade." I snatched the card from the boy's hand. "That's none of your business." I began to study hard while being up late at nights. The same thing happened the year that followed.

Johnny peppered students with spitballs all morning in the classroom while we took tests. The test was almost completed as I sat in my seat. The students were still being bothered by Johnny while I looked at them being hit. In a matter of seconds, a spitball brushed across my face. In no time, I got up out of my seat and lifted up my desk and threw it at Johnny as the leg on the desk grazed Johnny on the right side of his forehead while it knocked him up against the lockers. Blood spewed up against some of the lockers. The classroom was stunned as the girls started to scream. I pumped my arms and looked at my scrawny muscles. I was in awe of myself as I watched the blood trickle down Johnny's face. He looked at me in shock. I was soon being jerked by the arm. Mrs. Parker came out of nowhere while her anger appeared, and she pulled me to an empty desk. She said, "Carroll, what is wrong with you! I want you to sit right here while we take care of Johnny." An angry look came on my face. Blood still poured from Johnny's face. "Well, young man, I'm afraid you are going to the principal's office for this. I looked up at the clock while I sat in the principal's office. The clock struck three, and the bell rang.

My parents continued to argue about money as my dad looked for work. My mother and father always made sure that we would attend church. A new suit of armor on me for church pleased my mother very much. While my parents got ready for church, I would play with my dad's old army equipment that lay around the apartment. While we sat in the church, sweat soaked big black Reverend Baker's face as he stood in the pulpit. He said, "I want to speak to you this morning about a man! This man was no ordinary man! He was the son of slaves! There was something terrible that was going on in the village that was frightening all of the people, and there had to be something done about it!

"Battles were taking place all of the time. Yes, David knew what he had to do! Now David was just a small adolescent who was directed by God to rid his people of an oppressor. Before the giant Goliath had a chance to react, the stone from the slingshot was slung with such great force it impacted on the giant's head. He fell to the ground dead. David had killed Goliath." In that moment, I woke up quickly from sleep while in church.

Mrs. Parker stood up; with a stern look on her face, she began to pass out the report cards. The names were in alphabetical order. Mrs. Parker looked over at me and said, "Carroll Durham." I approached Mrs. Parker and reached for the card. The card said that I had failed once again. It was at this time my dad decided to join the navy.

There were soldiers that stood at the gate in full military dress. They had on white hats with dark blue coats and blue pants. Their shoes shined as bright as the sun. They also had on clean white gloves with their .45 pistols strapped on their sides. I looked at the soldiers once again and noticed how straight and tall they were. They both approached my dad's car to ask him some questions. My dad pulled a card from his wallet and showed it to the soldiers. Both of the soldiers looked at the card very carefully.

They told him he could enter the gate. My dad told me that they were marines. He said, "These are the toughest guys in the military. They go out ahead of everybody else when battle takes place." "What do you mean they go ahead of everybody else, Dad?" "What I mean, son, is that they are the first soldiers who are usually shot when a battle takes place." I remembered seeing the marines on TV. Were these the men that got off the assault boats to go on the beach? All of them would be in a straight line across as they charged the enemy. It seemed like they weren't afraid to get killed as bullets went past them and also went into their bodies as they fell and continued to get to their enemies with machine guns in the mountain.

At my first military base, an amiable young white boy named Jeff had become my best friend. We would be together most of the time. We would pretend to be soldiers as we played in the woods. The woods were very quiet on this particular day. The birds chirped as different other animals scampered around in the woods. On this particular day, Jeff and I decided to bring along a little food with us in an ammunition box. We had a canteen of water strapped around our waists. We also had a wooden rifle along with us as company. We were quite a ways inside the woods. I held my finger up to my mouth and said, "We have to be quiet because we are on a mission. The enemy will hear us if we make a noise, so we have to be quiet." Then Jeff said okay.

All of a sudden, there were some dog barks in the distance. It started to become louder and louder. The sounds became harsh barks as we got closer and closer. I looked ahead as my eyes widened. A pack of wild dogs jumped out of the bushes some distance ahead of us. The only thing that went through our minds was to run with all our might. We decided to run on a trail in the opposite direction. The dogs started to gain ground. The dogs were several yards behind us.

We continued to run and not give in. I threw away the ammunition box as the dogs stopped to sniff it. They tried to open it to no avail. We continued to run as we gained more ground. The dogs soon abandoned the ammunition box and got back after us. Jeff slowed down. He had gotten tired. I stopped and waited for him to catch up. Jeff gasped for his breath. Jeff opened his canteen and drank from it. I began to drink from the canteen that I had.

Right in front of us, about one hundred feet away, appeared a small stream, which had a little waterfall on the left bank. The dogs found our scent once again. They looked up the trail and saw us. They did not hesitate to continue the chase. Jeff and I looked at the swift-moving stream in front of us. A raft appeared that floated toward the bank. The dogs were right up on us when we jumped for the raft. The rifle fell out of my hand as I clung to the raft.

In the new integrated classroom, I began to study my schoolwork in earnest as my grades in the different subjects started to creep up from Fs to Cs.

My dad's orders came to transfer to another base. The new housing unit called Dog Patch fit the description for the enlisted men who lived there and worked at Camp Lejeune, North Carolina. One day, I walked over to where some boys were playing hide-and-seek in the playground. All of the boys stood still and looked at me as if I were something strange. One of the boys, who looked like Eddie Hascle, yelled out and said, "You're it!" The boy had a wide grin on his face when he looked at me. The boys started hiding behind a few of the trees that stood near one another. There were only about four trees in the little park area. I began to chase the boys. I ran toward the trees where some of the boys were hiding. It was luck that the trees were kind of close together. Then I started to show my quickness. A boy would throw the fake one way and go the opposite direction. I was sure to make a tag this way. The first boy was caught. He managed to tag another victim. One tree was about ten yards away, with a boy hiding behind it.

One of the boys' mother came out and yelled for the boy to come home. Soon I went after my next victim. I spooked him from behind a tree in hopes that he would go to another tree. The boy did what I wanted him to do, which was to my advantage. He soon was tagged. I got had one more victim. The boy ran toward the seesaws, and then all of a sudden, he stopped. The boy turned around and pointed his finger at me. He said, "My name is Chucky, and I am a judo instructor."

I didn't know whether the boy wanted to continue to play tag. In the meantime, the audience of girls started to form at the trees. One of the girls yelled out, "That boy knows judo! You better run!" I turned my head to see who said that. "He's gonna try and hurt you!" The next thing I knew was that the boy had grabbed my neck. I tried to trip the boy and break his hold. This effort did not work. The boy had managed to get a stronger and better hold around my neck.

The boy managed to get me on the ground. It was then I realized I was in danger. My effort to overcome the boy's grip was to no avail. Everything I tried didn't work. The girls realized that I really did need help at this point. The boy was cutting off my airway. A black girl named Patsy was the first one to run over to where I was being attacked. The other two girls followed her. Patsy started to pull my leg. She yelled over to the other girl named Gwen and said, "Girl! Grab that other boy's leg!" "Okay, I'll grab the other leg!" Both of the girls started to pull both of us in opposite directions. They started to pull my legs away from Chucky.

I really wanted the whole ordeal to be over with. "Turn me loose! Turn me loose! Turn me loose!" With the force of my yell and the pulling, this helped free me from the hold. I pulled myself off the ground and stood up to put my hand where my neck had been twisted. Everybody just stood around and looked at one another. I looked at Chucky and said, "Don't you ever try that again." Chucky looked at me and gave me a little smile. "I'll let you go this time, but don't you ever bother me again!" Chucky gave me another smile and licked out his tongue at me. The two girls still had me by the arms and shoulders. We turned and started walking back to the housing unit. Chucky went in the opposite direction.

CHAPTER 2

DOG PATCH

One afternoon while I sat on the porch, a yell was heard in the front of the complex. The husky-sized white boy yelled out, "Hey, boy! What did I tell you about that!" I saw a slender black teenager and two white boys who were having a confrontation. One of the white boys pointed his finger at the black boy. The white boy who pointed his finger then hit the black boy hard in his stomach. The other white boy slapped him across the face. Other blows followed and made their marks. These boys were much bigger than I was. There was nothing I could do. As the black boy slumped down to the ground, one of the white boys said, "Don't you ever do that again, nigger, or we'll kill you!" The boy hit the ground, and I could see blood come from his mouth. He held his side in pain as the boys kicked him as hard as they could. The boy went limp as the other boys taunted him as they walked off. I heard the sighs and moans as the boy lay on the ground.

Another incident took place from the corner unit directly across from where I lived. This was the unit where the Doberman pinschers lived. A rumpled middle-aged white woman along with a slender white man came out of the unit with the Dobermans on their leashes. The dogs pulled on the leashes as they gasped for air at the same time. I could see where the dogs chewed on furniture while the door was open to the unit. The lady could barely hold the dogs back. In the middle of the compound, two black males who seemed homeless walked toward the woman with the dogs. With hate in their eyes, the Dobermans noticed the black males right away. Their barks began to turn into growls. When the men looked at the dogs, there was astonishment in their eyes. As they passed by, their barks got louder and the growls got meaner. The dogs sensed the men were scared. The dogs broke loose from the leashes the woman had in her hand. The men realized they had to run for safety. The playground that was in front of them across the parking lot would be the safest place for them to get.

With a burst of speed, the men ran toward some swings on the playground. The swings were high off the ground. The men jumped on the swings with the dogs on their heels. The men started to pump the swings with a sense of urgency. The dogs jumped up and snapped their jaws to no avail. The men were much quicker getting out of the way of danger. The dogs continued to jump up at the two men. The woman ran behind the dogs as she tried to pull them back. The dogs got tired. They decided to go to the other side of the swing set and sit down. They were exhausted. Their tongues hung out profusely as saliva dripped. The woman was able to get to the dogs while they took their rest.

I walked through my room one day and saw a pile of military toys in the middle of the floor. In the corner, there were two duffel bags with locks on them. Some of the toy soldiers still had little cakes of dirt on them where they had been out in the field. The toy soldiers were beat up along with the little army trucks that were mixed in.

To meet children from different parts of the world made me feel how different I was when I was in the new classroom. These were a different kind of people who lived at this place called Dog Patch, a few miles from Camp Lejune. In the fall of 1962, I was thirteen years of age. It was an age to be reckoned with. I knew that something was on the horizon but didn't quite know what it was. To live in the South took on a different atmosphere at my age. The move from a military base in North Carolina to farther south was quite a contrast. Sumter County was a rural area of the South. It was just a small town named after a confederate general who was part of the Civil War. Fort Sumter was the shot heard around the world. The fort was located outside Charlestown, South Carolina, in the harbor. This was where the Civil War had begun. Sumter was in central South Carolina. It reminded me of the Western towns that I would see on the television, except there weren't any horses or wagons in existence.

My dad got stationed in California at Camp Pendleton in San Diego. I missed him at this period because we were together a lot up until this time. He got attached to a marine corps division that accommodated hospital corpsmen. The day he left was a tough moment in my life. The house I stayed in was a shanty. My grandfather lived there for several years. His wife left him and moved to New York City as a domestic worker.

My grandfather never served in the military. He worked at the air force base outside of Sumter, which was called Shaw Air Force Base. He worked at the officers' club as a cook in the kitchen. He was a burly kind of guy, weighing about three hundred pounds. He was overweight for his height, which was about five feet five. Even though he was a big man, he was all muscle. He attempted to go to college. This was back during the early 1900s when very few blacks went to college. He decided to leave South Carolina for the steel mills of Pittsburgh, Pennsylvania.

My grandfather lived in Pittsburgh for a while. He started his family while he worked at the steel mill. My family admired him because he was a mentor while my dad lived in San Diego. My dad was an enlisted man who didn't make that much money. Being in the navy was much different than being in the army during World War II, while he was single. My dad had a family to support now. California was a long way from South Carolina. I would only see my dad about fifteen days per year, and that would be when he got leave. I made friends while I lived in Sumter. My school grades in the sixth grade were outstanding.

My confidence had risen to new heights. I would continue to play combat with my new friends. I began to become interested in guns. There were some black boys I met in the neighborhood who owned BB guns. They were brothers. I had a BB rifle that I earned while I sold Christmas cards. One of the brothers' names was Willie, and the other brother's name was Butch. I noticed them one day while I played with my toy soldiers in the backyard. They had their BB guns with them.

They looked to see if they could find some birds near my grandfather's house. I noticed one thing about a BB gun, and that was it was hard to kill a bird with it because the BB would get lodged in the bird's feather even if you had a clear shot. The bird would often fly away after being hit. This frustrated me when I hunted for birds with my BB gun.

I discovered my grandfather kept a .22 rifle on the back porch in the corner. The rifle was for protection. I needed a better gun to hunt for birds, which was something that appealed to me. My grandfather would often take a nap after a day's work at the officer's club. I took advantage of this opportunity. There was one catch, and that was to get hold of the ammunition, which I needed. Where was the ammunition located? There was a hallway that led to the back porch. There was a chest of drawers that was in the dark hallway leading from the back porch. There was a hung light that was right in front of the refrigerator across from a chester drawer. This would give me some light so that I could see. In the chester drawer, there was a small drawer, which was at the top. I opened the small drawer, and there was a small box that contained ammunition. The small cartridge box was about two inches long. I opened the box, and there were the bullets that I needed. While no one saw me, I got the bullets and put them in my pocket.

The brothers were still hunting in the woods nearby. I picked up the rifle off the back porch and loaded it while I walked out of the house without being seen. I joined up with the boys, who were hunting with their BB guns. To stalk birds was no easy matter. It had to be done with stealth. I did not want to get close to the brothers in the small wooded area that was close to a residential housing area. At first the brothers didn't seem to notice that I had a .22 rifle. The weapon was kind of crude, with its wooded grip and stock. The barrel was about a yard long. I heard the pops of the BB guns go off.

All of a sudden, I noticed a robin about fifty yards inside the tree line. It was perched on a branch which was about five feet off the ground. I got in a prone position close to the ground. I proceeded to aim. My breathing slowed as I watched the bird in my gun sight.

Without hesitation I squeezed the trigger and put the rifle in action. The next thing I knew, the bullet met its mark. The bird fell to the ground. I ran to look at it. The bird's head was completely gone. The other boys ran over to see what I had done. They were surprised. The bird lay limp. He had no life left.

My grandfather was still asleep in the house. Butch said, "You took that bird's head off." I looked at the brothers while I walked away. The boys said, "Where are you going?" I felt the few bullets in my pocket. I turned around and told them I had to go. My grandfather would have been upset if he had found out that I had gotten the weapon. While I walked back to the house, a roar of jets flew information across the sky.

My mother had given up her job at the state department in Washington DC and felt she could get something comparable at the air force base in Sumter. I learned that the air force would play an important role while I was in Vietnam. To live around a base of this kind gave you a sense of patriotism. From time to time, I would see the air force guys come to town. A lot of them would live in the area. The housing was affordable, and they were close to the base. The base itself gave you a sense of security. Just to hear the jets roar overhead made me feel proud. To have my mother work at the base would be an honor to me.

In the fall of 1964, I was promoted to the ninth grade at Saint Jude High School in Sumter, South Carolina. For a boy who had lived across the tracks, I had moved up. The neighborhood was middle-class as the whites moved out. My teenage life was about to take shape. After I was successful in middle school, my dad noticed I had become a better student. My grades started to drop again in the seventh and eighth grade because my dad was not around to monitor my progress. I missed my dad very much.

My mother decided to write the president of the United States to find out why she hadn't gotten the job as an accountant at the air force base. She received the letter she looked for from the president. She began to work for the air force base because of President Nixon.

I was impressed with the Catholic school. My father took me to visit the school one day. We arrived at the little compound, which consisted of three buildings that held about ten classrooms.

My father said, "You see that building in the front of us? That is where the priest stays. His name is Father Randall, and the building to the left behind the chapel is where the nuns stay."

While I watched the civil rights movement on television, it was well under way. Martin Luther King was the leader of the movement. It would take me about thirty minutes to walk to school. To get across the tracks, you had to beat the train. One day, I barely got across the tracks. I and the train were in for a race, as I barely won the race as I held my books in under my arms. At this time, blacks were not allowed to go to the library along with the hotels and restaurants that were in existence. I walked past a cluster of poor whites that lived in shanties near downtown.

A desire to please girls as a teenager started to be of some importance to me. My dad had finally saved up enough money so that he could move our family out of my grandfather's house. The house that he found had a tin roof and shingled sides. It was a white house with three bedrooms.

There was a field near the school where the boys would play football. It was close to the size of a football field. One day after school, some boys decided they wanted to play tackle football with us boys from across the tracks. The teams began to form up. At this time, I decided to play defense, which I had grown to like from living across the tracks. My endurance started to pay off. Being quarterback was a leadership position, which I played across the tracks. To play defense was just as powerful a position. We tossed a coin in the air to see who would get the ball first. The boys from the new part of town would get the ball. My side kicked the ball off. What the other side did was to a reverse as soon as the ball was caught. The player they decided to give the ball to was the biggest player on their team. The big, burly boy's name was Billy.

Billy said, "Okay, guys, let's form a wedge. I'm going to run somebody over." I could see that Billy was a hard runner. He ran like a bull. I ran around various defensive players. The gap came, and I met Billy head on. I lowered my head and wrapped my arms around his body. I could feel Billy's knees as I tightened my grip on his body. It was a clean hit. Billy was lifted up in the air a good five feet. He hit the ground so hard that he turned the ball loose. His arm hit the ground so hard that it scraped against the ground. After he landed, I could see that he was hurt. The arm started to bleed. Billy lay there for a while. I came over to see if he was all right.

I asked Billy, "Are you all right, Billy?" Billy responded in pain, "Yeah, I'm all right." When this happened, the other team said they were ready to go home. Everyone was in awe at what had just happened. I attempted to lift Billy up, but he just wanted to lie there for a while. He was in so much pain. He was in a lot of pain as he winced. We became friends, but it was something both of us would never forget.

From time to time, I would wash windows for a drugstore downtown. As I washed the windows, I noticed a sign in the window across the street, with an old man in a picture with a big red, white, and blue top hat on. He had on a top coat, along with a pair of red, white, and blue striped pants. He pointed a cane in the air. He also had a long white beard, which looked like something from Simon

Legree. The old man shouted on top of a wooden box, "UNCLE SAM WANTS YOU! I felt like this man really wanted to get his point across. This old man really seemed to mean business. I began to think about me being in a military uniform. The picture had an aura of purpose that I felt. To me the idea to have a uniform on was important because my dad wore a uniform.

High school was taking its toll on me. My grades started to fall from As to Ds. I was ready to move on to a life of adventure and excitement, which I felt wasn't really there in high school. There was an episode when I had taken an interest to play basketball for Saint Jude. I would play some sandlot basketball when I was not on my job downtown. The previous year, the team had made it to the finals. That was as far as the team got. The team would practice in an abandoned church that was on the school grounds.

Another gym to play basketball was located. The facility that was agreed upon by the staff at Saint Jude was a historical black college in Sumter that had a basketball gym. The college was kind of in a remote area across town. You would need transportation to get to it. Transportation would be a problem because of the availability of a vehicle.

The trips to practice started to get dicey. It would be dark when we walked through the white neighborhoods to pass through to get to the college campus, where we would have basketball practice. We as a group of black boys together could pose some trouble if we were looked at in the wrong context. It was a fact that we went through a white neighborhood at a time when there was unrest. As boys, we didn't quite understand about the way we felt when we would go through the white neighborhoods. I felt it was best for me to stay out of trouble because I didn't want my parents to worry about me.

Practice had been kind of long on this night for us, and the fact that we didn't have any transportation made the night seem even longer. We finished practice and were on our way home. There was a corridor of houses that appeared right before you got to the college. These houses were the old colonial-type homes, where white affluent families in Sumter lived. There was also a gas station that was just beyond the colonial homes. Sometimes I would have a little change in my pocket to buy some candy to hold me over before I got home. We would stop by the gas station just for that purpose. As we approached the station, there were some white attendants that were on the inside of the facility. Everything seemed to be normal, except one of the men seemed to be looking at us in an odd way.

One of the men who had a rust-colored shirt with a black cap on along with a Southern drawl in his voice said, "What do you boys want?" I looked up at him and responded, "I want to get a bag of potato chips." The man reached for the chips. I reached in my pocket and paid the man for the chips. I put the change back in my pocket when one of the boys burst out the front door and started running. With all the commotion and reaction, I didn't know what was going on. The next thing I did was start to run right behind the boys. I turned around and saw the man go behind the counter. He pulled out a gun to my surprise. I then began to run. The man began to load the gun. He came to the door and started to run after us. He said out loud, "I hope you boys haven't stolen anything!" I ran as fast as I could. The man would have to shoot me in the back if he decided to shoot the gun. I slipped into the bushes for cover. The silhouette of the man was seen from the street light.

The other boys were ahead of me by about twenty-five feet. At this time, the boys were about a good block from the gas station. I continued to peek through the bushes to see where the man was located. The man just stood there while I saw the silhouette of the gun in his hand. He put a hand over his eyes to see where we had gone. The man soon went back into the gas station. He gave up the notion to chase us. Soon I came out from behind the bushes and yelled to the boys ahead, "Hey, guys, he's gone back in the gas station!" All I wanted to do at this time was get home. Combined with this event and transportation problems, I decided to give up on basketball.

My parents always struggled and argued about money, which didn't feel good to me. I did not want to be a burden on my family. I began to think about the army recruiting station across the street from my job as I continued to use the squeegee to wash the store windows. The old man on the poster called to me. "UNCLE SAM WANTS YOU!" It echoed in my head. I knew that my options were limited after high school. Graduation was beautiful as I received my diploma at the graduation ceremony. All the students were happy as their parents looked on at the small senior class of about twenty-five.

There was an incident that made me want to pursue a relationship with a girl that I met at a high school graduation party for seniors who were still in town after graduation. The party that I went to was given by a girl in my graduation class. Her name was Brenda, whose father was the only black dentist in town. A classmate's sister was at the party. This particular classmate's name was Ann. She was one of my best friends from Charlestown, South Carolina.

I approached a quaint brick home, which stood out in the community. The house appeared to be a little castle to me compared to the house I lived in. It had a screened-in porch along with a driveway that was alongside the house. I could hear some commotion of people in the backyard. These were the postgraduates who milled about in the backyard at the cookout. I rang the doorbell.

I waited at the door until someone arrived. Brenda answered the door. Brenda always had a broad smile, with her white pearly teeth showing. Her hair was fixed neatly on top of her head. She invited me in. "Hi, Carroll, come on in, everybody is in the backyard. Come on back so that you can join the rest of us." We walked through the living room.

"Aren't you glad that graduation is over? I just wanted to get it over with so that I can get on with my life."

Brenda looked back at me and said, "You and me both. So what will you do, Carroll, now that you graduated?"

"I almost didn't graduate, there were a few courses that I didn't pass. I'm thinking about joining the military."

"That's a pretty big step."

"I know, but I feel like this is something that I want to do."

"Boy, you got some nerve."

The decision was an easy one for me to make. My dad was in the military, and he liked to travel to different places. The idea of the military had been conscious with me all along. To go to Vietnam weighed on my mind. I knew what I had to do. We went through the kitchen, and Brenda proceeded to open the backdoor to the yard where everyone waited. The first thing I noticed was a new face in the crowd, which was a female that I couldn't keep my eyes off. She was with Beth. The girls in my class admired me and gave me my due respect. My charm was an attribute that had become a part of me. I walked over to where Beth was. I would not let a pretty girl get out of my sight if I could help it.

Why did I have butterflies in my stomach? She was what the brothers would call a redbone in black Southern vernacular. She was what you would call a pretty redbone that stood out in the crowd. She just seemed so dainty to me with her pink blouse and light green shorts on. She had nice brown-colored legs and a different sort of hairstyle that also caught my attention. She stood near the grill. I was about to get a hot dog off the sizzling barbecue grill and said, "How you doing?"

She looked away embarrassed and whispered something into Beth's ear, who was another one of my classmates. I guessed she was kind of shy. Beth came over to me and pulled me over to where her sister stood. She wanted her sister to respond to me. Beth said, "Darlene, this is my classmate Carroll. My sister is sort of shy. You'll have to forgive her, Carroll." Darlene then said, "I'm delighted to meet you." I gazed into her eyes. "Now what did you say your name is?" Beth nudged her sister toward me. "My name is Darlene. Now what is your name?" I felt good that we started to communicate. The ice had been broken.

"My name is Carroll. How do you like the party so far?" She smiled. "This is an okay party."

"Well, I'm glad you like it. I guess you came all the way here from Charleston to see your sister graduate?"

"Yeah, I wanted to see Beth graduate and see what Saint Jude was like."

"I've never been to Charleston before."

"Maybe you could come there sometime."

"I'd really like to get away from the place."

"Where would you go?" She had a puzzled look on her face.

"I don't know. I'm going into the military."

"Oh, that seems like that would be something you could do. I like to see men in uniform. Are you going in right away?"

"I don't want to be drafted. I want to volunteer. If I volunteer, maybe I won't have to go to Vietnam. I'm ready to get out of here and make some money. I don't want to waste any time. I'm going to the recruiting station next week."

"So when am I going to get to see you again?"

"I'll have to get some money and see what I can do." It would not be long before I would see her again. I asked her to write her address on a piece of paper. She quickly got a small piece of paper and wrote her address on it. She stayed on my mind.

An air force recruiting station was located behind the drugstore where I worked. The small brick building was divided by two glass doors in the middle with one door that said U.S. Navy Recruits, and the other door said U.S. Air Force Recruits. Inside the windows in front of the blinds on the windowsills were cardboard replicas of an air force and navy soldier. The sailor had a duffel bag on his back, looking up at a ship, while the other picture had a pilot standing by a jet airplane. The replica of the pilot appealed to me because it was different from the sailor. I chose to go in the door where the pilot replica was because of the air force base that was located near Sumter.

I wanted to present myself well. I opened the door to the office and saw an airman who stood up with his back toward me. He fingered through some files, which were in a metal file cabinet. He heard the door open. He then turned around. His demeanor appeared to be friendly as he pushed a little bit of his black hair to the rear of his head. He looked at me and smiled. "How you doing, son? You can pull up that chair up to the desk over near the window." I did what he instructed. The airman sat down in his chair at the desk.

"I'm interested in seeing about joining the air force." The airman looked down at his desk and then made eye contact with me. "Oh, you are. I guess you're at the right place, but right now, we have filled our quota. We are not accepting any more applications."

"Well, I guess I won't be joining the air force."

"Son, I'm glad you stopped in, but we just don't have any more room right now." I walked out of the office and looked at the old man who pointed the cane.

I entered the army recruiting office. An army recruiter sat at the main desk. A small sign on his desk said Recruiter Paul Smith. There was a chair that flanked the side of the recruiter's desk. The army recruiter behind the desk greeted me. I looked at his army uniform, which had a few medals and an insignia on it. The white recruiter had close-cropped hair with a few drips of perspiration that came from his narrow face.

"Is this where I sign up?"

"Yes, this is the right place to sign up for the army. Now what can I do for you?"

"So what do I have to do?"

"Well, there are a few things that we have to do, and that is get the paperwork you will need to get started."

The day had arrived for me to leave for Fort Jackson. The departure would be from the recruiting station right there in Sumter. I was given instructions to come to the recruiting station to be sworn in and leave for the processing center at Fort Jackson. I arrived with the necessary items for the trip. There was a white boy that I recognized while I stood in a group with some other boys. I had seen this white boy before in the neighborhood. He had sandy brown hair and brown eyes, who was kind of stocky but shorter than I was. The boy was disheveled. He had on a purple shirt and brown pants, which looked wrinkled but clean. He looked like he was in Sumter all his life. He seemed to be very friendly and talkative. He said, "Hey! Homeboy! My name is Jimmy. I seen you somewhere before."

"Yeah, I live on Oakland Avenue."

"Yeah! That's where I live, right before you get to downtown Sumter. It's a little small house on the corner that sits on some bricks." It was that section of the neighborhood where the poor whites lived. The house was in bad shape. I would pass the house to come downtown. This house had a front porch that had a torn screen door, which looked like it was about to fall down.

I introduced myself. "My name is Carroll, and I'm ready to go to Fort Jackson."

"So I guess we'll leave at the same time, homeboy. The recruiter told me to come down here and be ready to go. It looks like a whole bunch of us will be going to Fort Jackson. Somebody said that's where we will get our uniforms. I really need me some new clothes. They got a uniform just for me. I'm tired of Sumter. I'm glad I got a homeboy with me. At least that way you will know somebody." A military bus drove up with a military bus driver. "I guess this is our ride to Fort Jackson." Inside the building, the recruiter announced, "Everybody going to Fort Jackson, I want you to come with me so you can get seated on the bus."

We started to move on the bus with our few belongings. There were also some other boys already on the bus. The bus driver stood up. He said, "Okay, I want everybody to get on board so we can get to Fort Jackson. Make sure you take your bags and find a seat." We put our bags over our heads in the compartments. The ride was silent most of the way to Fort Jackson as some of the boys told a few jokes. The bus entered Fort Jackson as I watched the sentries at the main gate of Fort Jackson.

The bus pulled up to what appeared to be a depot. There were four soldiers with Smokey the Bear hats on who waited near a building as the bus moved in a driveway. The soldiers outside looked intently at the bus as the bus came aligned with them. The bus came to a stop as the doors opened. One of the drill sergeants came on board the bus. His voice became loud as he cursed the recruits who sat in their seats. He told us to get off the bus. We grabbed our bags in an instant. The other drill sergeants waited on us as we got off the bus. As we got off, each of the drill sergeants would curse and shout at us. "All right, shit birds, you ain't at home no more, so as of right now, you all belong to us, shit bird!" One shouted in my ear, "Do you understand what I'm saying, recruit!" The only thing I could think to say was, "Yes, sir!"

"Now I want you all to hurry up and form a line and drop your bags here because you won't have use for them where're you're going."

Soon the recruits were in the presence of some barber chairs, which were lined up about twelve abreast, with barbers motioning for the troops to get up in the chairs that were being emptied as fast as they were filled while hair fell and covered the floor. This came as a surprise. The recruits accepted what happened. A look in a small mirror was brief as you heard the barber shears do their job.

The recruits stood in line again to be prodded and poked by medical instruments, along with the different series of shots that had to be taken in each arm; the injections numbed our arms with pain. There was a series of necessary paperwork that had to be signed and completed in order for us get our pay started.

One of the first things the recruits would receive would be a duffel bag to hold all the army gear that they needed. I looked across the warehouse and saw about three or four rows of tables extended throughout the warehouse with bins behind them. There were different kinds of green equipment to be retrieved. There was one drill sergeant who said, "All right, recruits, let's line up so you can get the designated items that you'll need." These items consisted of all the equipment that new recruits would use, including pairs of dress and khaki uniforms, boots, shoes, belts, service caps, wool coats, underwear, and handkerchiefs. There were gloves, neckties, raincoats, along with utility shirts, shoes, socks, towels, wool trousers, and undershirts. The ID tags were given out later.

The chow hall that we ate in looked similar to an indoor bunk house with a kitchen that served hundreds of men. The cooks wore white in a serving area where we picked out various breakfast foods for the day. The day had come to night, and everyone seemed to be settled into the World War II barracks, which sat up on a hill that was called Boot Hill. One of the drill sergeants that had been with us most of the day would be with us while we were in the barracks. He would make his rounds to see if everything was in order. It was time for all of the lights to go out after our evening meal in the mess hall. I found a bunk in the right aisle. It was a lower bunk in the middle of the barracks.

The lower bunk was to my preference. I made up my bunk. All corners in the bunk were tight. In front of the bunk, there was a footlocker to put your military clothes in along with brass insignia and other items, which included socks, underwear, and other necessities that we picked up from the PX, along with a partial pay. The shower stall was located at the end of the barracks, where you could get in and out in a matter of minutes while they were vacant. The barracks were divided into two floors, along with a staircase located on each end near the entrance. About thirty or forty recruits were on each level, with a room for the drill sergeant. The fireman's watch had already been set up for the night. The shifts would be divided up during the night to start guard duty.

The drill sergeant informed us that we needed some rest because tomorrow would be an eventful day. Some of the new recruits messed around with the belongings they got from the PX. I noticed a slender-built white boy in the bunk on my right. I gazed at the boy for a short while. He gazed back. I stood up to get that last stretch in for the night. Somehow the new recruit felt threatened by my movement. He jumped up and got in my face as if he were the drill sergeant. "Who the hell you staring at, boy!" A small crowd gathered around us. With the recruit being so close, I pushed him back. The next thing I knew, we were wrestling and tussling. We each tried to get a grip to keep each other from getting the upper hand. The first thing I did was grab his legs and lift him up in the air so that I could body-slam him to the floor as soon as possible. He hit the floor with a thud.

It had happened in a matter of minutes. I looked at him while I was on top. Everyone looked on. I said to the recruit, "Have you had enough?" He said, "Yeah, you got me, man." I slowly got off him, and we went back to our bunks. There was no ongoing anger, just a development of respect.

I told the boy my name and held out my hand. "My name is Carroll. How you doing?" He did not return the favor. "My name is Peter, and I'm from Boston. You know something, you are pretty strong." There was no hesitation in my voice. "Yeah, you might say that." It seemed like the soldier wanted to have a conversation with me. With animosity in his voice, he said, "Do you know that black senator Brooks in Boston? I dated his daughter. She's a nice girl. We went out a few times."

"So! What do you want me to do, give you a medal!" I had heard about this senator on the news. All I wanted to do now was get some sleep.

The next six weeks would be a time of tested endurance. The harassment by the drill sergeants didn't bother me that much because

I wanted to get through basic training. There had to be some pressure involved in being a good soldier. The order of the day was set in motion as the straight and narrow drill sergeant appeared. He said, "I want you all at attention in front of your footlocker and look straight ahead. Don't look at me, keep your eyes straight ahead. I'll be watching your every move!

"Maybe one day you'll have your name tags on your dress uniforms, ready to graduate on the parade ground, but for right now, you're all mine. We will be in your face! Do you understand what I'm saying!" Everyone at once said, "Yes, sir!" He repeated it again. "What did you say!" Everyone was in unison: "Yes, sir!" He walked over and faced one of the recruits. "I'm not an officer! I'm a drill sergeant! So when you address me, you address me as drill sergeant, now let me hear you!"

"Yes, Drill Sergeant!"

As a matter of fact, my name is Drill Sergeant Brown, as you can see on my name tag, but you all will still call me drill sergeant. Do you understand that!" The recruits said in unison, "Yes, Drill Sergeant!"

"So don't forget that, and we'll all get along! I'm here to make soldiers out of you, and that's what I'm going to do if you pay attention. So listen up! These next six weeks is going to be a test to see if you all can make it through this boot camp. So let's get ready to go to chow so we can get our day started." After chow, we went to the exercise yard. The exercise yard was not far from the chow hall. The exercise yard was set up like a little arena; it had a platform, which the drill sergeant was on to lead the exercises.

These exercises consisted of jumping jacks, running in place, sit-ups, push-ups, and stretches. The pride in me began to take shape in basic training. It was a challenge to prove to the drill sergeant that

I wanted very much to be the best soldier in the platoon. The hot summer added to the tension of basic training in mid-July. Every day you would see different advanced platoons on a march going to the exercise yard. The difference in the growth was seen as these troops passed by. To be advanced meant a lot to me. It was that next stage that I wanted to get to.

I had the ability to go home on the weekends. The recruits who lived far away would spend a lot of time on pay phones to make contact with relatives and friends who lived in such places as Florida, New York, Pennsylvania, Boston, Maine, and other places out west.

A lot of guys would spend the weekend drinking because of the beer gardens that were located on the base, where you could buy cheap beer or what they would call 2.0. These beer gardens always gave off the beer odor as the troops would pass these facilities when they were on the march. The troops would form groups and hang out together according to where they were from. The beer pitchers would be located on all the tables as recruits would gulp the beer down.

One night, a recruit attempted suicide as we saw the medics come and take him out of the barracks. At unexpected times, the drill sergeants would wake us up for inspection while we were still half-asleep. We would have to unlock our footlockers. The brass and insignia for the uniform had to be shined and put in proper order along with dress boots and belt buckles. Our free time was given to us to take care of these matters.

Our dog tags would jingle while we ran. My body started to get firm and chiseled from doing all the exercises.

I didn't know what happened to my request to go into the field of communication. All I knew now was that my military occupational specialty would be infantry. This also meant that I was a rifleman. My face was glum when I peeled potatoes on kitchen patrol.

We were on a march when the drill sergeant picked up the pace and said, "I don't know, but I've been told Jody's got your girl and gone, am I right or wrong!" Then it would be an echo of the same refrain. We would say, "You're right." He continued the refrain, "I don't know, but I've been told Eskimo pussy is mighty cold. Sound off one, two, sound off three, four, sound off one, two, three, four! You're right!" Rain poured on us as the days went by. Drill Sergeant Brown would still get in your face if he felt you were out of line.

We ran through twenty sets of tires as we felt the exhaustion from the obstacle course. To climb the wall with a rope tired you even more. The mud splashed on our faces as we ran through the little man-made ponds. The one-mile course we did in four minutes made you breathe in labor. Recruits threw up their breakfast as I saw them fall off the wayside.

It was a dark night on a back road in an opened field where a small juke joint stood out. I drove my dad's '55 Oldsmobile as I got close to the juke joint. The cars were parked all over the place. It seemed like everyone had their headlights on. With my fresh, new army uniform on me, I got out of the car and entered the dark cinder block building. I pulled out a pack of cigarettes and lit one up.

A juke box was located against the wall in the back of the building. Guys and girls milled around it as some people danced to the music. I decided to join the crew who was around the juke box. I recognized Bobby from boot camp. He was on the other side of the juke box. As the music played, I went over to say hi to Bobby. I tapped him on the shoulder. The next thing I knew, he swung on me and caught me with a punch square on the jaw. I staggered back, trying to gain my composure, when Bobby lunged at me again with a knife he pulled out of his pocket. I caught the arm where the knife was.

We wrestled to the floor. I landed on top of Bobby. My fist was cocked and ready to take Bobby's head off. Some friends from Saint Jude caught my arm before my fist landed on Bobby's face. They pulled me back and tried to console me. I was blindsided. One of the boys from Saint Jude said, "Come on, Carroll, let's get out of here. You can go over to my house." A few other boys held on to Bobby as he tried to get at me one more time. I was furious as I felt where Bobby hit me. The Saint Jude boys continued to pull me out of the joint.

Wounded, I stumbled back to the car in a daze. I took a lemon from my friend and began to suck on it while on a couch. I walked out of the house to get some fresh air. Soon, I began to get sober. Bobby stood in almost the same spot while the music played in the juke box. "Hey! Do you know the name of that song playing?" He turned to face me. The next thing Bobby knew was that a straight right landed square on his left cheek with a force that knocked him to the floor. His body went limp. I stood over him for a minute and walked out of the joint.

The Greyhound terminal in Sumter was small and uncluttered for the people to get ready for travel in the late sixties. I looked good in my uniform, which fitted me to a tee. My dress shoes were bright black as they glistened. The ride on the bus took an hour or two, with various people from South Carolina on it. I was the only soldier on the bus. I smiled at the little old ladies and small children, who made the trip with me. You could smell the fried chicken and ham sandwiches that were packed in little small bags.

Charleston's first appearance was that of a sedate-looking place with magnolias, sleeping willows, with manicured lawns. The bus entered into a bus station that appeared again to be well kept like the one in Sumter. I hailed a cab as I stood in the midst of the bus terminal. The Southern yellow cab that I took went through the residential streets as I arrived at a bungalow residence two stories high. I looked up at the address while I paid the cab driver and got out of the cab.

I walked up to the residence and looked around. The lobby had a few pieces of furniture, which were in the lobby. I walked up the stairs that was in the building. The piece of paper I had in my hand had the exact apartment number. I knocked on the door until a small, petite black middle-aged woman arrived. I could tell from the resemblance that this was Darlene's mother. She said, "Hi! You must be Carroll. Come on in! We've been expecting you. How was your ride on the bus?"

"It was okay."

"Come on in and sit down." I walked over to the couch that was located in the middle of the living room, where I sat down. Everything was neat and in place. There was a rug in the middle of the dark wooden floor. "So how do you like the military?"

"It's okay, I only have a few more weeks, and I'll be going to advanced infantry training." A smile came on her face. "Oh, that's so wonderful! What do you plan to do after that?"

"I believe I'm qualified to go to communication school. After I get out of the military, I will use the GI Bill to go to college." Darlene entered the room as I stood up. She had on a pink see-through blouse and a purple-looking skirt on. The first thing she said was, "You look nice. Did you get my last letter? You know I got your letter. I wasn't writing anybody else." I gave her a smile as we both sat down on the couch. Darlene's mother walked out of the room. "Well, what do you want to do?" I just shrugged my shoulders.

"Let's get out of here!"

"Where are we going?" She jumped up and left the room. She came back with a small purse in her hand. "I know where we can go. I just want to get out of here." She grabbed my hand and forced me to my feet. I was somewhat surprised as she pulled on me in earnest. "Ma, we'll be back a little later!" Darlene's mom replied, "Okay, be good. I'll be right here."

The little restaurant, coffee shop, and soda fountain establishment wasn't that far from where Darlene lived. We entered the quaint restaurant hand in hand. A booth was empty across the bar soda fountain. I asked Darlene, "Would you like to have an ice cream sundae or something?" The juke box was playing some Marvin Gaye in the back of the little restaurant. A melancholic look was on Darlene's face. When she turned toward me, her face lightened up as I walked from the fountain with two ice cream sundaes. I sat down with the sundaes. The sundaes were packed with ice cream and cherry on top. Darlene took her cherry off and pushed it against my lips. She then said with a smile on her face, "You are a cherry, aren't you." In a terse manner, I said, "What's that supposed to mean?"

"So what have you been up to?" she replied.

"Oh, nothing much, I'll just be glad to leave home. My mother is okay, but sometimes she gets on my nerves."

"My sister is with her boyfriend, down at the beach. I'm so tired of the beach. I go down there all the time. I just wanted to get away from that house so I can do what I want to do."

"You're only in the twelfth grade, it won't be long before you'll be out of high school."

"I just want to have some freedom, like my sister. Come on, let's go for a walk." We held hands as we admired the scenery of old Charleston, which was very beautiful. The looks of the Civil War was still present in this old town. Some of the armaments from the Civil War were present. I started to feel something for Darlene.

I walked Darlene to the door of her apartment door. "I guess I'm going to have to say good-bye now." Darlene stood at the door and closed her eyes as if she would get a kiss from me. I grabbed her in my arms and got close enough to not give her a kiss. I pushed her away and went down the lobby to call a cab. The cab arrived. I told the cab driver to wait for me and that I would be right back. I ran back up the stairs and knocked on the apartment door. Darlene opened the door and stood there with her shirt partly off, where her breast could be seen through her blouse. I planted a passionate kiss on her lips as if there were no tomorrow. She pulled me inside the door as it shut.

The day was sunny without a cloud in the sky. D company was honored for making it through basic training. My family sat up in the parade stands as they watched the formation being inspected. The troops stood in line, showing what they had been made into, and that was being as sharp as possible. They stood in line formations, arm's length apart, marking time with their M.14s. They soon came to at ease. We stood in front of the officers and drill sergeants. The brown khaki uniforms would be in contrast to the green lawns of the parade ground, which was a magnificent sight. The ceremony was impressive as the civilians looked on at the brand-new soldiers. The adults in the stands seemed to be subdued as they watched their sons or fathers go through this stage of the military.

I was now in an infantry battalion, which was for ground troops to be sent overseas. The large dining area was attached to a large kitchen in the new facility. You could see large silver kettles, which had temperature gauges on them to monitor the heat of the food. The cooks would be seen with their all-white uniforms on doing their duties, with a few KP soldiers in the back who continued to peel potatoes.

I entered my new room and noticed a soldier unpacking. He had already changed into his work fatigues and was sorting his civilian clothes. The handsome black soldier turned around as I stood in the room. He was a little taller than I was but still a young-looking man. His appearance was of a neat manner. His hair was short and had a few curls, which complimented his handsome brown face. He introduced himself. "Hey! How are you doing? My name is Jefferson. I'm from New York City." I said to him as I put duffel bag down, "I'm okay. How you doing, brother? My name is Carroll. I'm from Sumter, about forty-five miles from here. I used to live in DC, but now I live down here."

"I'm from Brooklyn and ended up here at Fort Jackson because I got drafted. So I guess I'll have to deal with it for now. I'm married and need some money for my family. I don't have any kids yet, but this is the first time me and my wife have been apart. New York is a long way from here, so I guess I won't be going home often. Hopefully, I can get stationed up at Fort Dix, New Jersey, once I finish my training here at Fort Jackson.

"I just want to get this whole thing over with, so I can get back to my lady. Go ahead and get your things put up because we'll probably be seeing each other quite a bit. I'm getting hungry. As soon as I finish this, I'm going to get some chow." He seemed like a pretty nice guy. His demeanor was that of a New Yorker as he expressed himself. The relationship between me and Jefferson would be purely roommates. The soldiers that were married carried themselves a little differently than the recruits who were single.

Advanced infantry training consisted of a lot of forced marches and getting familiar with light infantry weapons. Sometimes you would get picked to go to different kinds of advanced-weapons schools, which were available. You had to be able to deal with all kinds of elements under combat conditions if you wanted to make it in the infantry. It was a part of the military that was looked down upon. I wanted to approach it with the right attitude now that I was in the infantry. Even though you were looked at as a grunt or what they call a pig in the mud, it would be something that I had to get through.

The use of the pugil sticks was a contest you would learn as you were in the midst of AIT. It was a contest between two recruits with large sticks that had cushions at each end to absorb the blows that were going to be thrown. There was a cup that was strapped around your private parts. The idea was to outlast your opponent and keep him from knocking you down. You would move around in a made-up ring similar to boxing. This training took place at a little camp complete with a small set of bleachers. The bleachers were where you could observe the duel or form a circle so you could get a better look. The rugged Drill Sergeant Baxter said, "Hey, Durham, I want you to pick someone out to fight." I stepped into the circle and pointed to the biggest opponent I could find in the unit. He looked big, like he wanted to be wrestler.

I figured this recruit was big, but he would also be slow. So what I wanted to do was keep this giant recruit away from me as much as possible. I gathered all my equipment and got prepared to fight. I walked into the ring to start my feint and jabs while being quick on my feet. The object was to keep him off balance. The opponent came at me with a ferocious swing. His swing was as wide as I was able to counter with my inside jabs who met their marks. It surprised me the jabs got through. I started to back my opponent up. I ducked and escaped his blows. He got frustrated because he could not catch me. I made it through the rounds without being knocked down or knocked out. The rest of the recruits cheered me on. The match was soon over. I believe that I had gotten the best of my opponent.

One day in the cafeteria, I noticed a black recruit who ate his meal all alone. I soon got my tray of food and walked over to where the recruit was. "Hey! How are you doing?" The slim freckled-face, light-skinned black soldier replied, "Oh, I guess I'm doing all right for a square."

"I guess that makes the two of us." We both laughed together and then exchanged names. "My name is Robinson. You see my name tag, don't you?" He looked up at me and laughed.

"My name is Durham." I gave him my hand, and he responded.

"Where are you from, Durham? I don't live too far from here. I live about forty-five miles from here." On occasions, Robinson and I would hang out together when we got a little free time. We would go bowl, play pool, or go to a movie. Robinson had a real nice basketball game. Sometimes we would just walk around Fort Jackson to get away from the barracks. We had become good friends.

It was payday as I stared at the paycheck in my hand. It would be in a safe place under my pillow in the barracks. I woke up the next morning and looked for the check under my pillow. The check was not there. The check was gone. It must have disappeared sometime when I was not in the barracks.

That morning I saw my roommate Jefferson and told him what had happened. We both got dressed to go out to formation. I explained to him what had happened. "Guess what, somebody stole my paycheck. Did you see anyone messing around in our room?" Jefferson had a puzzled look on his face. "I didn't see anyone in here. I came in kind of late last night from playing pool."

"Well, I guess it just got legs and walked out of here." That check would have covered my expenses to go to Charleston. I managed to call Darlene and tell her that I wouldn't be able to come and see her.

There were some weapons that we would learn while in a ravine where you could shoot down at your target in the forest of Fort Jackson. One such weapon was the M.60 machine gun and the .50-caliber machine gun. The targets would often be small to medium-sized trees. These targets were about two hundred yards out to get the maximum efficiency. We would handle these weapons with an instructor present. He said, "Pretend that the trees are your enemy." When I shot the .50-caliber machine gun, I got down in a squat position while I sat on a stump. It was a monster as I pushed down the butterfly trigger to make it jump in place as it spouted out the bullets, blowing away tree limbs. The .60-caliber machine gun was different than the .50-caliber machine gun. I raised the weapon waist high to get maximum offense. The .60 was like a loud sewing machine that shook in your hands as branches and limbs would continue to fall to the ground. There was a little bit of nervousness as I managed to get through it.

There was a class where I learned how the .45 operated, along with assembling and disassembling the weapon. It had to be done in about a minute until I got proficient at it. The .45 was bulky to me as I fired it along with the recoil. With the M.16, it just took a matter of repetition to shoot at the target to become a marksman, which was next to being an expert.

One morning, I looked at a list of names on the bulletin board. It said for me to report to the .81-millimeter mortar range. There was another list for communication school. My name was not on that list. I told Robinson that I would not go to communication school. The weather was still warm, so I would report to the station with all my necessary equipment. The station was located up a little hill. There was a little house that made it look like a small-built barrack. The other side of the barracks was adjacent to a ravine. This area was also fenced off. I could see several mortar barrels pointing downrange, set up in a line. On the other side of the door, there was a slot with a name in it. Inside the slot, there was a name that said Sergeant Riley. There were recruits who saw the .81-millimeter mortars down the ravine.

The door opened to the cabin like building. A medium-built sergeant with a Smokey the Bear hat on opened the door. He had sandy hair, with pressed fatigues on. A pad was in his hand. The first thing he said was, "All right, men, I want you to go down the hill and get ready to get some instruction on the .81-millimeter mortar." He continued to speak as they walked down the small hill. "Some of you will be assigned to a mortar platoon, and some of you will go to the infantry units as a grunt!

"I'll be back here in the states, teaching greenhorns like you how to operate this weapon called the .81-millimeter mortar. So I want you to get the wax out of your ear and listen up!" I felt the anxiety as I looked at the four mortars that were lined up facing out to their pretend target. "All right, gentlemen, this is going to be a test. As you can see, these mortars are basically set up and ready to go. There are several pieces that are attached to this weapon. As you can see, the mortar tube sets in a base plate, which holds the tube in place. There is also a sight that is attached to the side of the tube so that you can look down range."

Sergeant Riley stepped out in front of the mortar tubes. He moved to the right side of the mortar we looked on. "I want everybody to take a good look at the inside of the mortar tube. You see that firing pin sticking up?" The sun had made the pin visible. Everyone was leaning down to look into the tube. "Gentlemen, that pin is what ignites the rounds. We don't have any rounds here today. The rounds are called the .81-millimeter round. We don't use live rounds on this range." He then pulled out a piece of paper. "Come close so you can see how this round looks." The round looked like a small rocket. "This is how the mortar looks. It has a set of fins at the bottom. As you can see, there are several charges that also exist on this round. At times, some of these charges will be discarded to help with the distance of the round. These rounds can go as far as two miles in almost any direction in 360 degrees.

"The least amount of charges you have on these rounds, the closer the round will land near you. You have to turn the barrel up with the little lever to the side. It has a killing radius of about thirty-five yards in circumference. The shrapnel will angle up like a cone. In other words this is a deadly machine if used properly!" Sergeant Riley pointed to some candy cane poles, about five feet high, that were sticking up in the ground about thirty yards out, lined up in front of the mortars. Two of them were about twenty-five feet apart. The poles were red and white, like candy stripes.

"You see those two poles? They will be set up about twenty yards out and about ten yards away from each other. They will be lined up with the mortar. The test is for you to get those poles set up in less than five minutes so you can line up your target. I'm going to show you this one time and one time only!" Sergeant Riley walked out to where the poles were. He looked back to see if these poles were lined up with mortar. He also looked out in the direction of the wood line, which was about five hundred yards out.

He walked back to the mortar tube. He looked through the sights of the mortar. He turned the lever to align with the poles as he looked through the sights. He traversed the tube with the lever to adjust the mortar more to its target. He also cranked the tube up a little bit from the lever that was attached to the tripod.

This made the tube stand up a little higher. He told us to look at the sights so we could see the poles and where the hairline was supposed to be positioned. Sergeant Riley looked at me and said, "You see how that hairline is an equal amount of distance from those poles?"

"Yes, Sergeant!"

"That's how I want it to look when you set up those poles. I'm going to take those poles down to see how fast you can get an aim on your target." Sergeant Riley jogged out to retrieve the poles. While he came back to the mortar, he said, "I want the rest of you troops to stand back and watch as I time you." He laid the poles down on the ground. He looked at my name tag and said, "All right, Durham, I want you to go ahead and get started. You will be graded on your performance.

"This will determine if your primary job will be a mortarman. So get those poles lying down, and I'll let you know when to get started. Remember, you have less than five minutes!" I looked back at the other recruits. Sergeant Riley walked over to the middle mortar. He chose this mortar for me. He said, "Come over here, Durham, and grab those poles." I followed Sergeant Riley over to the mortar with the poles in my hand. Sergeant Riley looked at the watch on his arm. I looked down at the mortar. Sergeant Riley looked at his watch again. "On the count of three, I want you to go! One, two, three, go!"

I picked up the two poles and ran out about fifty yards out where a pole should be planted. I looked back to make sure the mortar was aligned with the first pole that I planted it in the ground. Due to nervousness, I slipped down after I put the first pole in the ground. The next pole was planted about twenty feet away. I ran back to the mortar to see how close my target would be. I looked for the hair in the scope. I knelt down to look into the scope. I needed to traverse the knob to get the further alignment that I needed. As the knob turned, Sergeant Riley spoke, "Your time is up, soldier! You didn't stay within the five minutes that was given to you. You failed the test soldier!

"Your primary job will be a rifleman in the infantry. Sorry, you were just a little slow, son." It was as though I failed once again like when I was in elementary school in Washington DC. I dropped my head as my heart sank. To add to my wound, my hopes to get out of being a rifleman was determined. Then to add insult to injury, Sergeant Riley asked me my name once again. "Now what is your name, soldier?"

"Look at my name tag. Can't you read!" Sergeant Riley stared at me with a menacing look on his face. The sergeant walked away and jotted down something on the pad that he carried.

CHAPTER 3

ARRIVAL IN VIETNAM

The Tiger Jet with about two hundred troops on board didn't feel like a pleasure ride. I knew now that this was serious business. The attractive stewardesses accommodated us as much as they could. Their presence made me feel somewhat comfortable. The speed of the plane increased as it made its way up in the clouds. This was supposed to be a routine flight to Vietnam with a plane full of troops destined for Vietnam. I saw California disappear in the distance.

I only knew one guy on the plane, and that was Robinson. We both were quiet and reserved on this flight because we did not know what to expect as we sat by one another. I slept as Walter Cronkite showed images of Vietnam on television. I saw myself in the midst of combat as I stood over the bird that was killed in Sumter while the image changed; I stood over a dead Vietnamese soldier with his head blown off while I stood over his body with my M.16. The bump of the plane woke me up as it continued to bump up and down in the air pockets. I said to Robinson, "When are we going to get our weapons? I do not have the slightest idea."

The flight to Alaska was through heavy clouds as we rumbled through them. The plane would manage to keep up its speed. Anchorage, Alaska, was a military weigh station on the way to Vietnam. The stewardesses would pass by us and ask if we needed something to eat or drink. I did not have an appetite because of the meal I had eaten at the Oakland air base.

I leaned over to look out the window again, and there began to appear land through the clouds. I saw icy patches scattered around along with land masses. The plane started to descend. We were over Alaska about to approach the runway. The land seemed so sparse and remote. The plane began to circle again. The drag of the plane began to come into play. After the plane hit the runway, it rolled into the airport. Robinson was still asleep. I nudged him. "Wake up, Robinson, we're at the airport."

The plane rolled to a halt. The captain appeared in the aisle and said, "Gentlemen, we'll be here a few hours for refueling until we get under way, so get off and stretch your legs and look around until we get ready to depart." The airport seemed to look isolated and gloomy. It just wasn't that much to look at. We made the best of the situation. The Anchorage airport looked like a big museum with a few stores and artifacts that came from Alaska, which was the attire worn by the Alaskan population. We were dressed for the climate in Vietnam, which was hot and humid. As the hours went by, we walked up and down the airport. There still was a form of nonchalance about us. It wouldn't be long until we got back on the plane. The captain walked up to us and said, "Let's mount up, troops, it's time to go."

There were clouds in the sky that day that seemed to add to the drama that was about to take place. To leave Alaska felt like something had been lifted inside of me just as the plane got under way.

The captain said, "Fasten your seat belts, men, so that we can get under way." Soon the plane lifted off the tarmac. This time the destination was the Republic of Vietnam. Would we come as liberators or intruders? I didn't know how my partner from New York felt at this time, but he was in awe just like me. This would become a long flight. We traveled a route over the Pacific. I soon fell back to sleep. The remainder of the Pacific flight moved along with no hitch. The idea of the plane falling off into the water was the last thing on my mind as I looked at the vast ocean.

The hum of the plane engines felt determined to make its destination. I would drift to sleep off and on. I got a little to eat from what the stewardesses served us. I thought about Darlene, who I had met at high school graduation. My orders were still in the big manila envelope that I had bought on board the plane. I looked at the manila envelope in front of me, which was still in the pocket of the backseat. I picked it up just to look at it. It was still sealed. Right in the front in big letters, it said Confidential. That was the way I would keep it.

The approach of the airplane to the country of possibly no return had come into view. The land of Vietnam came into view. The canopy of the land caught my attention. There was lush green forest scattered throughout the territory. There also appeared to be houses scattered about. The most visible scenery was the charred look of gray land in patches that were very visible. It seemed like every few miles or so the land would look like this. The rice paddies also began to stand out as people in black pajamas tended the rice fields with water buffalo in sight. It looked like a country in war. I looked over at Robinson and said, "I guess we're in Vietnam." The plane began to descend. The air fans on the top panel began to cease.

I looked around the plane to see the expression on the other troops' faces, to see if their expressions had changed. There was some somberness along with sternness in their facial expressions. The mood changed from the nonchalant. The stewardesses seemed to be in a jovial mood as they looked at us to see if we were okay. The plane's engines made their final cooldown as the plane continued to make the descent.

I began to see military artifacts as the plane approached the runway. This gave me some relief to know that there was some support at hand. The structures at the airport seemed like a military staging area where troops would be. I could feel the jolt as the big metal plane hit the runway once again. The plane began to taxi into the airport.

A lump came in my throat as the plane came to a halt. The appearance of the straitlaced Captain Buford standing at the door made you mindful about what was about to happen. He said, "All right, men, it's time to go." Everyone grabbed his gear. I stepped off the plane as the morbid heat hit me in my face. I rubbed my nose to the odor like a mixture of olive oil and vinegar.

Everybody filed out in a line formation as if we were about to be executed. The line got divided. My duffel bag was over my shoulder as I held onto the manila envelope. A captain waited on the tarmac until everyone was off the plane. I looked around at the gun posts that surrounded the big base camp. The soldiers were perched up in their guardhouses with sand bags that surrounded them waist high so that they would have enough cover to see their target. They had on their helmets with MP insignia on them.

Vietnamese civilians were on the base camp doing their duties. The Vietnamese seemed eager to serve the American soldiers. The women wore black pajamas and white tops. The men wore a different type of garb.

From where we slept that night, we were led out to the flight line where the planes waited. I felt naked with the duffel bag as far as necessities were concerned. The smell of diesel fuel filled my nostrils. There was also the appearance of other troops in the area. The units moved along in formations. The appearance of the big C-130 started to put things in more perspective. The big green aircraft imposed a big figure. It looked like it had been around for a lot of dust offs.

The plane's big mouth opened as we approached it from the tail end. It got filled with the multitude of troops. There were a lot of harnesses on the plane so that we could latch ourselves in; there were also personnel there to help us load on. They had on jumpsuits with earphones attached to their heads. I didn't notice any weapons other than the ones the door gunners had. The plane started its takeoff; in a while it was soon in the air. My partner, Robinson, would soon separate from me. I could see Robinson on the other side of the plane. The question now was what division we would be assigned to.

It would have been nice if we could go to the same outfit. This would be one journey that I would have to take alone. Being a foot soldier was what I had to deal with now. Everything I worked for in the past six months boiled down to this. I would finally get involved in combat. The fear had not really emerged for me yet. It was my duty to God and my country to do what soldiers do, and that is to kill the enemy. I just wanted to get to my unit. I wanted to be able to fit in.

The plane started to bank. It was as if the plane was looking for something. The plane found a landing strip. The plane went into another bank and dove. I could see the land again. There were still burned areas that were present once more. The plane got closer and closer to the battlefield. There appeared to be a small military compound beneath the plane. This compound had military structures that started to appear. The military barbed wire circled the compound. The plane glided into the small air strip. As the hatch opened wider, the military compound became more visible.

The plane managed to stumble on the bumpy runway that threw dirt and rocks as the plane landed. The plane came to a halt. At the opening of the hatch, there appeared a noncommissioned officer who was probably a platoon sergeant. With his high, rough voice, he said, "All right, men, let's start to move off this bird so we can get you all to headquarters." All the troops got off the plane in formation. He said, "Gentlemen, you are now in a forward combat area. This is Chu Chi. Here you will be divided up unless you are on the buddy system. All right, men, the main headquarters area is about two clicks up the air strip, so let's double-time so we can get off this air strip." I was ready to run because it kept you in good shape. This time I would run with a purpose. I looked over at the other troops with a slight smile. I truly enjoyed the run because it was in preparation for what was to come.

Robinson had gone to another unit for his stay in Vietnam. Now was the time for me to meet another comrade. The area we arrived in had small Quonsen huts that were aligned to one another. I approached one of the huts and looked around. There was a platform with an American flag located in the middle of the compound. There were cutoff jeeps and trucks used to carry supplies and troops. There were also ammo boxes on some of those vehicles. The sergeant then said, "All right, men, we'll have to divide you up so that you all can be able to get some sleep tonight. Lately there's been a little activity at this compound."

CHAPTER 4

INITIATION INTO THE FIELD

As night drew near, an adjustment would have to be made in this new barrack where I would sleep for the night. There were certain personality traits that drew me to a particular soldier. There was one soldier that stood out. His name was Stewart. He was a big, burly black trooper. He was black as night. He seemed so relaxed and comfortable. He said, "Man, I can't wait to get to my unit so that I can kick some ass." His appearance was such that he was somebody that needed to be taken seriously. Yet he was friendly and loved to joke. He befriended guys right away. There was this one white kid whose name was Andy. He was slim and small in stature. He would walk around the barrack and display his cigarettes, which he felt he needed to show everybody. The guys would go outside around the barracks to smoke. I wasn't concerned about smoking now because I started to think more and more about the field.

While I sat on my bunk, I observed all the items that were needed for the field like my toothbrush, toothpaste, soap, and other small items that were necessary. All of a sudden, Andy ran back in the barracks. He whined and cried as he said, "This guy took my cigarettes." Stewart, in astonishment, turned around and said, "Who the hell took your cigarettes?" Andy said, "It was one of those white guys outside." He was laughing about it. Stewart wasted no time to get outside the barracks.

I looked toward the door to see what was going on. Next thing I knew was that someone hit the ground with a thud. I ran to the door to see what would happen next along with some other recruits. The soldier who hit the ground got up with a slow movement as if he wanted to stay down. Stewart punched the soldier twice again. He fell to the ground. He kicked the soldier several times in the ribs. You could feel the impact of those army boots meeting their mark while the soldier grimaced in pain as the boots made contact with his ribs. It was like something that really caught him by surprise. All I knew was that it was not me who got pounded. Stewart was a strong man. He was more than a match for anyone in the barracks.

Things grew quiet after the event. All of us headed back into the barracks while the soldier just lay there. Then all of a sudden, there was the sound of gunfire along with artillery going off. It didn't sound like it was that far away. The soldier who was hurt made it inside the barracks just before a rocket hit in front of the door. The soldiers who were still outside the barracks made their way back into the barracks in a hurry as they escaped other rounds that exploded near them. I felt helpless. I clung to the post on the bunk bed as the ground shook underneath the barracks from rounds that had gotten closer to us. I lay awake until I went to sleep.

All the recruits were up bright and early the next day. The incident from last night had been forgotten. I cleaned up around my bunk. My duffel bag was on the right side of the bunk. A sergeant appeared in the doorway, which was nearly blown away. Everyone looked at him. He said, "At ease, men, we had a little friendly fire last night. No one got hurt, thank God. We will have formation soon so that you all can get to your units, so just stand by until we call you for muster."

An impression came over me about the military and some of my comrades; it was about how the military would make you hurry up and wait. This time, the wait really meant something to me because this was one of the last departure points until we would go out into the field with our units. The sergeant came in once again that morning. This time he shouted, "All right, men, I want you to come out here in the yard to get information!" There were impressions from the rounds that hit last night along the side of the barracks. The sergeant then said, "Snap to it!" I gathered up my duffel bag while everyone moved out into the compound.

The compound was full of soldiers. The platform in the middle of the compound had a makeshift stand that had a megaphone on a podium within reach. There was a captain and a lieutenant who stood on the platform. A formation was being formed in front of the platform.

As we stood at attention, we were called to at ease. A list of names was being read off by a clerk who stood to the right of the captain and the lieutenant. He said, "Will you please listen up while your name and your unit are being called." I had no preference as to what unit I would be called to; all I knew was that I was ready. All that was on my mind was to get my weapon. The clerk began to call off names to two hundred soldiers who stood in formation in an anxious wait for their name to be called. Your unit was called and then your name. I heard different divisional names being called. I heard the Americal, the Twenty-fifth, the Eighty-second and Big Red One, along with a host of other divisions that were present in the region. Some soldiers would load onto trucks, while others would move on to other small formations with their platoon sergeant.

The clerk continued to call out names. Then it was my turn to be called. The clerk said, "Private Carroll A. Durham Jr., Echo Company, Second Battalion, Fifth Air Cavalry, report to your platoon sergeant!" A sergeant appeared to the right of the formation and said, "Carroll, fall out and follow me." He told me, "You're the replacement that we've been expecting." A sense of relief and discomfort came over me. Sweat came down my forehead. There was no adulation, but there was a sense of reserve.

I was finally going to my unit. I knew now I would soon get my weapon along with the other ammunition I needed. The sergeant addressed me again. "All right, let's go, we've got a helicopter to catch. Your company is about eight clicks to the south of here. We should be able to catch up with them in the next twenty-four hours." I noticed the sergeant had a .45, which was strapped to his side. I thought about when I learned to shoot the .45 back in advanced infantry training. It seemed so long ago. In reality, it was not that long.

Some other GIs and another sergeant were at the helicopter pad, getting ready to get on board one of the helicopters that had been waiting. I held on to my boonie cap and held my duffel bag while the big blade on the helicopter twirled. I got low so that the blade wouldn't take off my head. There was a little more assurance when I saw the two door gunners with .60 machine guns peering out of each side of the helicopter. I felt the heat of the engine along with the blade as it blew dust. The helicopter hovered a feet off the ground while I jumped on to hold on to a secure part of it while I kept my balance.

The helicopter began to rise at an angle. It rose above the tree tops pretty quickly. The ride was exhilarating. The eyes of the door gunners began to look out over the lush scenery of the bush below. The silence was still in the air among the men. You really didn't know what each of us thought at this particular moment. The noise of the helicopter and motion started to give you a little adrenaline rush. I looked below as my legs dangled from the helicopter. I wondered how much I was exposed. I looked over again where the two .60 machine guns were at, which bullets were encased in the guns.

The helicopter soon landed at an undisclosed area. There were some man-made barracks, which resembled half-made huts with sand bag roofs and openings on the side, which were on platforms. There was enough clearing for the helicopter to get in without hitting the trees. The arrival was friendly. We jumped off the helicopter while it hovered.

This was another departure point. It had gotten past midday. This area reminded me of an out post, which looked like it might have been occupied from time to time. The sergeant pointed us to an area where we would sleep. The handful of troops continued to depart the helicopter. We ran to the nearby compound. I still had my duffel bag with the new fatigues that I had gotten from Chu Chi. I had about three T-shirts and underwear with me. I had no idea where these items would get washed. Maybe I would find a creek or river to wash them in. I started to mingle with the other troops that were already there. They seemed the same as I was, just waiting there to get further orders. I claimed my cot, which was set in the middle of the hoochlike structure that I had entered. I noticed a blond soldier in the corner of the big, room-sized structure as he sat on his cot. Commissary items were located on the side of his cot. The military patch on his shoulder was from the Big Red one. I approached the soldier and said, "What's going on?"

He looked up at me in an odd way and said, "I guess I'm doing okay. Have you been here very long?"

"I've been here for about a day. What's going on around here?" The soldier stared at me and said, "There're a lot of gooks around here."

"I'm getting ready to go and meet up with my unit." The soldier looked at me and said, "You just got here?"

"Yeah, about twenty minutes ago."

"I'm getting ready to go on R & R."

"Where are you going?"

"I'm going to Hong Kong." This soldier must have been in Vietnam for a little while in order to go on an R & R. What I was really interested in were the quarts of whiskey that stood out along with the rest of the items that the soldier had around his cot. I said to the soldier, "Can I buy one of those bottles of whiskey?" The soldier looked up at me and said, "Yeah, you got any American money on you?"

"Yeah, I got a couple of dollars."

"Give me a dollar and I'll let you have one." I pulled out an American dollar and gave it to him. The soldier took the money and held it up to see if it was for real. "You don't have to worry, it's for real." I looked at the fifths of bottles that were assembled on the floor. There was Jim Beam, Wild Turkey, Southern Comfort, and a number of other brands. The Wild Turkey was the bottle that appealed to me. I got the bottle and inspected it and proceeded back to my cot.

A sergeant showed up and asked me, "Soldier, is your name Durham?" The sergeant looked at my name tag that I had on my fatigue shirt. "Yes, that's me, Sarge."

"In the morning, you'll get all your equipment so that you'll be able to go out in the field. So be ready." There was some gloom that came over me when the sergeant gave this information to me. Reality hit me in the face. I got some food from the mess tent. There was nothing else to do but wait for the morning to come. The sun was going down. My mind began to drift as I sat on my cot. I looked down at the quart of whiskey that I had bought from the soldier earlier in the day.

It was at this moment I cracked the seal on the bottle and proceeded to devour the contents as if it were my last drink. The harsh whiskey went down my throat with an uneasy taste as I grimaced. The decision to empty all the contents was my intention, and that is what I did. It wasn't long before I fell back on the cot. The empty bottle dangled in my hand. I was out like a light. The sun came up as my body woke up. The adrenaline rush had kept me in good stead. My eyes were bright. I hoped to have this effect for the rest of my stay in Vietnam. I wanted to be alert to make it through the next eleven months, so now was the time to get focused. My reflexes had to be sharp at all times. There was no hangover from what had happened the evening before. It seemed to me what happened last evening would be my initiation rites to get ready to go to the field. I gathered myself for my debut in the field.

The sergeant from yesterday appeared again. He told me, "I want you to come with me so that you can get your gear. You can bring that duffel bag and empty it out because you'll be receiving a ruck sack, so let's go, soldier, so that we can move out." I followed the sergeant out to a tent, which was guarded by two soldiers who looked like they had not been there long. It was an odd place to have ammunition. I entered the tent, and there were bins on both sides of the tent, which had crates of different kinds of weapons and supplies. It was almost like being in a candy store.

There was a limited amount that an infantry soldier could take. I looked to see what I was interested in the most. There was a bin of M.16s, one for grenades, .45s, machetes, bandoliers, with M.16 rounds already loaded into magazines. The magazines were something I checked to make sure all the rounds were there. I got five bandoliers of M.16 rounds. I picked up a flight vest and helmet that would be of some use to me. There was a poncho, along with a small blanket and shovel that would come in handy. I looked at the .45s and passed by them.

My interest was to have plenty of fire power for my M.16. I decided to get three grenades. I attached the grenades in front of my vest. One was a baseball type, and the other two were regular grenades. In the corner, there were crates of c rations and canteens. The c rations were in small cartons, along with a P-38 can openers. The food would last me for a few days at least. I looked over at the sergeant. The sergeant told me, "You'll get a hot meal in a few days."

I got all the necessary equipment that was needed for me to stay alive. The sergeant told me to get water pills so I could purify the water that would be used. He handed me a little packet of about two dozen water pills. I positioned all my equipment where it should be. The majority of my equipment would be on my back. It was about seventy pounds of equipment. I felt the weight of the equipment as I adjusted it on my back. The five bandoliers sagged on my shoulders and waist.

I turned toward the sergeant and said, "I'm ready to go."

"You sure you got everything you need?"

"I believe so, Sarge."

"All right, let's move out, we've got some people to meet up with. Your unit is only about five clicks from here." The Huey arrived with all the dust that kicked up as I waited to board it. The pilot and the two door gunners started to look more seasoned. The First Cavalry patches were more visible now. The guns on the helicopter were mounted and ready. I was weighted down when I entered the helicopter.

A few soldiers were already on the helicopter. The soldiers on the helicopter seemed to be weary. Their fatigues looked very used. Silence was appropriate at this time. I positioned myself so I could get comfortable. My M.16 was loaded with the safety on. I held a death grip on the weapon with confidence. Precautionary measures started to come into play. The helicopter started to rise. It seemed as if it were routine to the pilot. It wasn't a long flight. Soon we approached our destination. I could see the clearing near the wood line where the helicopter would land. There were sentries that made a four-corner perimeter, which surrounded the helicopter.

They all had their M.16s pointed to the outside of the perimeter. They were ready for some action if it were to take place. The adrenaline started to increase in my person. The helicopter began to hover. I jumped from the helicopter with the added weight that was on my back. I landed perfectly on the ground. As I looked ahead, I could see someone signaling for me to go in their direction. By looking around at the other soldiers, they started to form a little formation on the ground. They were headed in the direction that I would be going. I walked toward the signal caller with all the commotion of the helicopter in the background. The clip of rounds in my M.16 was now on automatic. The soldier who had signaled came into focus. He was a short, stocky built white soldier. I noticed the rocker under the three stripes on his shoulder.

He packed a .45, which I noticed right away. The sergeant had on a rucksack along with a green steel pot and a canteen of water on his side. He approached me with a smile on his chiseled face. He wore the military-style crew cut. With a gruff voice, he said, "Welcome to E Company. You're one of the replacements that we have been waiting for. Charlie has been active in this area, so we've got some work to do." He held out his hand. "My name is Sergeant Greely, we will be patrolling this area until we get further orders. So welcome to Echo Company. I want you to go join with the rest of the troops for now." I looked ahead and saw the troops who sat straddled along the road. It looked like a road that someone had been through before. The troops looked kind of worn out. My fatigue uniform was cleaner than the rest of the other soldiers'. It made me stand out. I still had a lot to learn while in the country. I knew also that I had a lot of time to do in the country.

Sergeant Greely said to me, "I want you to position yourself right behind the radio man or what we call the RTO. We've got about three more clicks before we take a little rest." Everyone was about four to five yards behind one another. I could feel the weight of the bandoliers, which attempted to cut through my sides. I also felt the weight of the grenades on my vest as I looked at them.

The backpack was a hindrance as I adjusted it on my back. A soldier muttered under his breath, "Oh, here's my replacement, a fucking new guy or what we call an FNG." The terminology disturbed me as I looked at the soldier with a glare in my eyes. This was whispered down throughout the formation. I approached the rear of the radio man as I heard the squelch of the radio. It was a loud squelch, which echoed throughout the jungle. My six senses got heightened as I stepped behind the RTO.

I looked up at the trees and along the tree line. I asked the RTO, who seemed like a nerdy kind of guy who wore glasses with brown scraggily hair, "Hey, have you seen any snipers in this area?" The radioman ignored what I said as if he had something else on his mind. Sergeant Greely approached us and said, "All right, men, let's saddle up because we got a ways to go if we want to find Charlie. He's around here somewhere, and we are going to find him." The soldiers were in a lax mode as they sat on the ground with weapons in hand. Some were in a prone position with weapons aimed out in the proper position. They started to rise and move along the open trail. I looked ahead to see what was in front of me. I fixed my eyes on the point man that was out front. The point man was one of the most dangerous positions for a foot soldier. I could see the point man about fifty meters out in front of the platoon. The point man would also have to be quick to pull back into the unit formation while he was being covered.

The radioman's main objective is to communicate with his radio. The radioman carried an M.16 along with his other equipment. I asked him, "Hey, radioman. What exactly is your job?"

"My job is to stay in contact with artillery and the airplane pilots."

The presence of camouflage was all around you as I looked at the forest. My head stayed on a swivel along with the strain as I carried my heavy equipment. To relieve myself of the unnecessary equipment would be a relief. I noticed some of the other soldiers didn't have the same amount of equipment that I had. The decision was made to discard the unnecessary equipment. We came to a shaded entrance in a portion of the tree line.

I knew absolutely nothing about these men. Yet they were a part of my unit. There were two soldiers that I noticed right away. One of the soldiers passed me as he looked for a position to settle in. A sullen, pale look of anguish along with strife was on his face. His fatigues looked dingy. He had a small cigar in his mouth. A large jar was cradled in his arms. The jar was full of human ears. It looked like they were preserved in vinegar. His M.16 dangled from his left shoulder. This came as a shock to me. This brought about anxiety in me that came as a surprise. There was also another soldier who moved from his position in the formation with a human skull attached to the top of his rucksack. The soldier with the skull had on a utility cap, which was frayed along with his worn fatigues.

The skull faced backward. These two men looked like zombies who were in a daze. I asked the RTO about the skull, and he told me that the Vietnamese were superstitious about human skulls, which would keep them away. I asked the RTO, "What else would he use that skull for?" A slight smile was on the RTO's face. "Sometimes the guys will drink beer out of it."

Was this really a part of war? Or is this what becomes of a man when he is in combat? This was another thought that would linger with me for a while. I wanted to be around men who were good fighters, not butchers. Gunfire erupted with a fury that caught us off guard. I turned to see where the gunfire had come from. I turned the muzzle of my M.16 to where I wanted to get a good look at my target in the brush where the rice paddies were. My first instinct was to get down low. I discarded my rucksack, which freed me so that I could get my M.16 on the target.

My rucksack would be my cover as I moved closer to a tree near me. Being near the RTO is a vulnerable position. I could hear the rounds pierce off the trees close to my position. Out of fear I got as low as possible with my head down. With my head down, I pointed the weapon toward the rice paddy as I sprayed M.16 rounds in the direction of the rice paddy, where I thought the enemy was, until the clip in my weapon was empty.

CHAPTER 5

GOING INTO THE VALLEY

I fumbled to get another clip into my weapon. There was a repeat of what my reaction was. Soon, the firefight was over. My first firefight took me by surprise. My reaction would be different the next time. To get to know the men who were in my unit was very important; it was something that had to be addressed. The toughest man in the platoon was the one I wanted to get to know, and that was the point man. To walk third or fourth man was hard enough. I wanted to know the point man a little better. Echo Company's point man was named Smitty.

Smitty was short in stature with an attitude. You could tell he had been in the field for a little while. Smitty was irritable and ready to explode at any minute. He walked back toward Echo Company from his point man position. He waved his M.16 and said, "Hey!

It's me! Don't shoot." There was a cigarette tilted out of his mouth. His mood changed. He walked up to me with a smile on his face, with the cigarette about an inch from my face.

He moved back and gave me a pretend jab with the butt of his M.16 as I moved to the side in a playful manner. He threw his cigarette down and got in my face once again. "How you doing, brother? My name is Smitty, and I don't take any shit! I'm really starting to get tired of walking these boonies. I'm getting where I don't really give a fuck! For one thing, it makes me feel like I'm looking for a ghost. You know Mr. Charles can be like a ghost."

Smitty pointed his M.16 in the direction in front of the formation. "Charlie will pop up his head from time to time to let you know he's out there. This is Smitty talking! I plan to go back to the world alive! I'll walk point a few more times, but it won't be much longer because I'm getting too fuckin' short. I don't know if I'm going back in one piece." He picked up the cigarette from the ground and put it back in his mouth. He looked back at the upcoming trail that he would be leading the platoon into. "Yeah, that's right, they call me Smitty, and I'm a hell of a motherfucker! So I would advise anyone to not take me lightly, not even the CO, because I really don't want anybody fucking with me! I go through enough shit as it is dealing with Charlie and these crackers! So I don't have to take no shit off any of those cocksuckers."

A tall black soldier named Harry appeared, with a boonie cap tilted to the side of his brown head and a blue and white scarf around his neck. He had a slight mustache, with a rumpled fatigue uniform on. His boots were fairly worn. His M.16 was loaded and on automatic. A sullen look was on his brown face. He looked at Smitty up and down.

He said, "Look at this little motherfucker! Ain't he short!" The soldier looked at me and smiled. He looked like he came out of the woods somewhere. He looked at Smitty and smiled. "He thinks he's the shit. Don't let him fool you. He's just one of those jive Negroes from back East. Really, there's nothing to him. I should give him a rifle butt to the mouth. He's just a short motherfucker who thinks he's tough." He seemed to have known Smitty pretty well because he talked a whole lot of trash about him. He asked Smitty, "Why the hell are you out there walking point? You 'bout a crazy motherfucker! Who the hell do you think you are? Audie Murphy or some shit? You know that Charlie will fuck you up out here." Smitty looked at the soldier in an odd way. Smitty retorted, "Look you bootlicking bama, who the hell do you think you are?" The soldier looked at Smitty in amazement, as if he needed to back off.

The soldier was amused by Smitty but not sure of himself as his expression gave him away. He appeared to be somewhat of a nuisance, but yet he could be tolerated.

Smitty got up in the soldier's face. "Ever since we been here, you've been a pain in the ass. Why don't you grow up and mind your own damn business." The soldier laughed it off and said, "Oh, Smitty, you know you like to walk point. That job was made for you. Plus you are a little short motherfucker, so go on out there and do your job!"

Smitty got angrier and angrier by the minute. I thought that in a few minutes, a fight would break out. Yet they seemed like they liked each other. A black-knotted boot-string band was wrapped around their wrists. I asked, "What do those black bands you have on your wrists stand for?" The tall soldier said, "These bands stand for black power, brother." He raised his fist in defiance. "This is black power! Power to the people! That's what we say back in Watts.

Just because you from Boston don't mean shit to me." They both began to smile at one another.

A picture of the riots came to my mind that I saw on television. There was a particular edge to Harry. Harry was a product of Watts, which stood out. Boston was also another part of America, where Smitty was from, that was affected by racial strife. They fitted the mole of two black soldiers that were affected by what had happened back home.

This really didn't help the situation that they found themselves in. The defiance would soon take its toll. I had been shielded from the riots because in South Carolina, I had not been a participant of the riots. I was shielded from those events because my dad was in the military and my mother worked for them also. My civil rights would be fought through other means, which was to kill as many Vietnamese soldiers as possible.

Sergeant Greely said, "Saddle up! It's time to move out." You could hear the equipment being mounted and picked up, ready to go. Everyone fell back into the two-line formation, with Smitty taking his position reluctantly out front. As he walked back to point, he mumbled to himself in protest. Harry walked back near the rear flank in his rifleman position.

I wanted to observe as much as possible about my comrades because these were men I would get to know very briefly. Just to concentrate on what was ahead was emotional. I earned my combat infantry badge in a short period of time. Maybe some of the greenness had started to come off. My courage still had to be tested because of the type of adversary Mr. Charlie was.

Right now, the main thing for me to do was to keep my composure and make sure it didn't tilt in the other direction. The canopy of the jungle seemed so real. It was a different feel being in a foreign country, with woods that were so much different than the woods that were back in the States. We passed by rubber plantations and rice paddies. The land seem so ancient but so real. I looked up in the trees again as we walked through the bush. The idea of a sniper who looked at you in his gun sight disturbed me as he looked at me through his sight in my mind. He was about to pull the trigger. The crackle of branches and bushes was heard as we walked through the boonies.

The enemy was the obstacle that had to be overcome. I felt the only way to do this was to become my own man in a combat uniform. I still would act along with my unit. Humping in the boonies started to play on my psyche. I had not heard from Darlene. Mail call started to be a part of the weekly routine. The mail would come in most of the time by helicopter. It was good anticipation to see a helicopter come in with expected mail. It was good to see the helicopter because of other reasons, which made the helicopter an important machine. It would drop items of importance that had a lot to do with survival, such as ammunition, more armor, and food or man power. I missed Darlene. I had a dream about her one night. She would be on the beach waiting for me with her arms in an embrace. I ran to her in desperation. I woke up and realized where I was. Even though I had a brief encounter with her after my graduation, she was still in my thoughts.

It seemed like every time the mail would come in, I would get disappointed. There were smiles on soldiers' faces as their names were called out for mail. It was an ache in my heart when I didn't get mail. I wanted another woman to acknowledge me other than my mother while I was in the field. There was also a feeling of not having someone care about you while you were in a strange country. There was also a need to have a woman near you, especially if you were a virgin. Being in a country seven thousand miles from home without a girl friend made me feel desperate because I never had sex from a woman.

There was always enough clearing for the helicopter to land and drop its supplies. The sergeant would always ask for volunteers to go out and retrieve the supplies. I always felt being around a helicopter would make you an easy target. At this point, to volunteer was not good. That's how I ended up in Vietnam. The idea of being vigilant had been so remote to me in the past.

Sergeant Greely said, "All right, we need a volunteer to go out and get the supplies from the helicopter." A helicopter hovered for about a good five minutes. Sergeant Greely yelled out, "All right, I said I need a volunteer to go out and get the mail, or I'll draft somebody to do it!" A few of the soldiers raised their hands. Sergeant Greely pointed to two soldiers. "All right, you two go and get that stuff off that helo so that we can get the hell out of here."

"We only have a little bit of time because not only are we after Charlie, but he's also after us. We have no time to waste, so move out!" The helicopter twirled with a lot of commotion as the soldiers were able to get to it and pull the supplies off. Echo Company was in a circle formation, which made a perimeter for the helicopters.

While in my prone position, I could see the red bag being moved off the helicopter. Maybe there was some mail in the bag for me. By now my gear was much lighter than when I first got to the field. At this time there were three bandoliers of M.16 ammo strapped around my shoulder and on my waist, along with my canteen and c rations. A boonie cap and fresh clothes were what was on me after two weeks. Along with a blanket and an entrenching tool, my M.16 stayed in my hand. I had two full clips that were taped together loaded into my M.16 on full automatic. This would make me much quicker.

The volunteers yelled out names that were getting mail. There was no letter for me as the final letter was handed out. Sergeant Greely looked at me and said, "Maybe next time you'll get some mail, Durham." A lump came in my throat as it dawned on me that I had not received a letter. There was an emptiness that I felt. I shook it if off to gain my composure. I would look at the other soldiers who got mail to see them smile after they got a perfumed letter from home. The smell drifted throughout the company. Sergeant Greely gave us a brief period to relax, but soon we would get back in the line formation to trudge through the woods of the area we were in.

Sergeant Greely said, "All right, men, let's saddle up, we got some ass to kick!" Sweat came down my brow. The mystery of the forest seeped into my conscious. A monkey made a loud shrill. All I wanted to do was get to know the terrain and look for all movement that was suspect in the forest as well as the thin underbrush that was mixed in with the scenery. This would always be considered as we walked through the terrain. The enemy's way to attack was on his terms. There started to be complaints among the soldiers of the fact that they didn't know why we were in Vietnam. Some would say we were here because we have to police the place up and the fact that this is not a declared war. A lot of times, the conversation between the troops would be trivial because we were so young.

The conversation among the black troops would often be about black power. You still would have to know how far to go with that conversation. I would think about my missed opportunity to be in communication. I always watched the radio operator because this was something that I also had trained on in boot camp. Being able to handle the radio was something that was important. Smitty would continue to complain about his position as point man. You needed fortitude to be a point man, or you would have to accept the consequences. The mortarman position was still fresh on my mind also. Sergeant Greely continued to make his rounds to see how we were doing.

Echo Company walked up on a riverbed when Sergeant Greely informed us that we would have to cross the river. He told Echo Company, "We will cross this river to see what's on the other side. Maybe there are some regular uniformed NVA waiting on the other side." This was a suicide mission to me. Sergeant Greely made sure everybody had everything secured. We secured our M.16 on the top of our rucksacks. Sergeant Greely gave the order. "Men, I want you to get in two line formations so that you can see one another in case someone gets into trouble!" I thought this was crazy but knew it had to get done. We proceeded into the water. For about half a mile, we used the American stroke, and all of a sudden, Sergeant Greely said, "All right, men, let's turn around." He proceeded to turn back. I looked over at Sergeant Greely in surprise and wondered why we were turning back. Maybe Sergeant Greely had a bad feeling about what was on the other side.

So everyone reversed their stroke and proceeded to turn back around. The ruck sack had posed no problem because it would float and would help your swimming. The challenge had been effortless. Everyone succeeded and made it back to the bank, where we had just left, with no fanfare but figured it was a mission accomplished. After we got back to the bank, Sergeant Greely told us to fill up our canteens. We dripped in wetness from the swim. Sergeant Greely told us to purify our water with the purifying pill, which made the water taste like iron. A grimace would come on our faces as we drank the water. Sergeant Greely said, "All right, men, we still have several clicks to go, so let's stay on the alert and be aware of what's around us." The squelch on our boots was evident.

We soon walked up on a creek. It looked muddy and marshy. Sergeant Greely yelled out, "All right, men, we have to cross this creek, so let's get moving. I really did not want to deal with any more water, but this was a small creek, and it had to be crossed. This water was dirty as we waded through it. We managed to reach the other side. Sergeant Greely yelled out to Smitty, "Hold up, Smitty, we need to slow down a little." Smitty slowed down and got in a crouch behind a tree. Sergeant Greely went around inspecting us and seeing if everyone was all right. The area the mud stuck to was from the knee cap down. The mud and water would soak into your boots.

There was an irritation in one of my legs. I checked the area where the irritation came from. There was a torn area along with blood in my bloused fatigues pants' leg. I pulled my bloused fatigues farther up my leg. I saw a slimy worm like thing on my shin, along with another one farther up my leg. They were leeches. I pulled them from my leg right away. I began to scratch the area where the small creatures had come from. Pus began to form. This was something I did not want to happen.

We got back into line formation. We continued on foot for about another five or six clicks. We approached another clearing with enough room for a helicopter to land in. I checked the condition of my legs, which were both affected. My fatigues turned a dingy green and started to stick to me. I pulled up my pants legs up again. Both my legs were blistered all the way up to my knee. This time it was jungle rot.

I walked in a daze. Sergeant Greely walked toward me. He tapped me on the shoulder and said, "Son, what is the matter?" I showed him my legs. He said, "Son, you got jungle rot." Sergeant Greely walked off as if nothing had happened. All I could do was wonder what would happen to my legs now. I hoped that my legs would not rot off. I could see an image in my mind of the medics taking my legs off. I soon snapped out of the illusion. Sergeant Greely came over to me again and said, "We should get some supplies shortly so that we can have something clean to wear."

The unit proceeded to set up a perimeter until the helicopters arrived. I got on one knee and inspected my M.16. A tall black soldier approached me from the side. The soldier was dark skinned and had a wide smile on his face. He was well built with pearly white teeth showing, along with his boonie cap tilted to the side. He carried a .60 machine gun over his shoulder, with ammunition dangling all around his chest. As he approached, I gave him a sneer along with a grin. He looked to be about six feet two, maybe 220 pounds. He had a physique similar to Muhammad Ali. I was glad he was on our side. He looked at me and grinned as if he saw something funny. I got up on my feet to meet this big black soldier that approached me. The soldier said to me, "I didn't tell you to stand up!"

I gained my composure and smiled. "I'll stand up when I feel like it!" The black soldier replied, "Did I tell you to stand up?"

"I'd like to know who's going to make me sit down, you and what army!" Then the big man replied, "Oh, you ain't gonna do what I tell you!" Then the soldier said, "Oh, man, I was just kidding you." A relief came over me because I didn't want to fight this big man. A smile came over my face because I didn't know if this GI was serious or not. All I could do was go along with the joke that was presented to me. The soldier just stood there.

He put down his armor and got in a boxing stance. He started to throw fake punches at me. I jumped back and went into a boxing stance. I put up my guard. A few more fake jabs were thrown by the big man. I responded in return because I was not to be intimidated with. He continued to throw fake jabs at me. The big man said, "What's my name?" He smiled at me. "My name is James." He decided to stop his antics.

"So where are you from, James?"

"I'm from Baton Rouge, Louisiana." The big man then extended his hand in friendship. I was glad that we didn't have to engage in a real fight. We both smiled.

"You can call me Durham." We hit it off right away.

I asked him about his M.60 machine gun. "Do you really keep that thing clean?" James looked at me in bewilderment. "Are you crazy! You damn right I keep this gun clean, or I'll be a dead motherfucker!" He showed me a little pouch, where he kept his small plastic bottle of oil and broken-down pieces of cleaning rod.

"Let me have some of that stuff."

He replied, "You don't have any of this stuff?"

I looked at him and smiled. "I'm no fool, of course I have some of that stuff in my backpack."

"You'd better have some of this stuff if you are going to be dealing with Sir Charles. You never know when Charlie is going to pop up, so you'd better be ready." I looked at his weapon, and there was not a hint of rust on it. We both looked at each other's weapons as we inspected them. I then said, "Well, I hope you know how to use that thing because we are going to need it when the time comes."

"What is your specialty?"

"My specialty is to kick ass and get back to the states."

I looked at the James again and smiled. "Okay, I believe you, brother!" I bowed down to him. Sergeant Greely then came over and said, "Well, men, I've got orders that we will be moving out to a place called LZ Rita.

CHAPTER 6

LZ RITA

Sergeant Greely then said, "Do we have anybody here with mortar experience?" I raised my hand and said, "I learned how to work the mortar in advanced infantry training. Sergeant Greely looked at me and said, "We might need your help at this new location. Do you know how to use the radio?"

"Yes, I know how to use the radio." Sergeant Greely put his hand up to his cheek and said, "Okay, let me think about this and chew on it for a while." The excitement ran through me. My ability to use the mortar would be challenged again. This time it would be for real.

A perimeter was set up to wait for the next helicopters to come in. Everyone was geared up and ready to go. While I waited for the helicopters to come in, I saw a couple of soldiers who carried certain parts of the mortar. I could see one soldier with a small tripod and base plate while the other one had the tube. It didn't look like the .81-millimeter mortar that I had trained on. It was much smaller. It just looked like a smaller version of the .81. This weapon was portable and ready for use, with a third man who carried the small rounds in his rucksack not far behind. I was anxious to get the opportunity to use the .81-millimeter mortar. I boarded the next helicopter. The helicopters came in one by one. They hovered for a short while and got on their way. The helicopter lifted up through the air. The remoteness of Vietnam became present.

It wasn't long before I could see a clearing; it looked like a little compound from the air. But as the helicopters got closer, the compound appeared bigger. A helicopter pad appeared right below us. There were bunkers, concertina wire, and artillery pieces that were positioned out beyond the helicopter pad. There were three mortar pits that were next to what appeared to be a

first aid station. There were also .60 machine guns located in between the four corners of the landing zone. There were four black trucks in each corner also mounted with .50-caliber machine guns on them. The helicopters settled down on the helicopter pad. I saw wooden pallets that had been off-loaded. They sat scattered around the helicopter pad. In them was ammunition that waited to be picked up. There were soldiers with different jobs on the helicopter pad to help keep the landing zone clear.

There were cut-off jeeps, which were called mules. Soldiers drove them around the helicopter pad to perform certain duties. While Echo Company off-loaded, we had to meet up with Sergeant Greely, who was in the lead helicopter with the captain. I could see Sergeant Greely motion to us to come to an area near the center of the landing zone. It was near a first aid station, along with a large bunker, which sat about two hundred yards inside the perimeter. Sergeant Greely waited for Echo Company to arrive. You could see our two line formations come toward where Sergeant Greely stood. All our heads were on a pivot, with a slow trot toward Sergeant Greely, while we carried our M.16s. We encircled Sergeant Greely with a certain amount of attention to see what our next order was; I couldn't help but look around and see the artillery pieces that stood out. Sergeant Greely began to speak with a cigarette, which dangled out of his mouth; he talked between puffs. "All right, men, we made it to Rita safe, so let's keep it that way. I have orders from headquarters that we will be here for a little while to give some support and do some patrols. So I don't have to tell some of you what that's all about. You know how that goes. Charlie is definitely in the area. So what I want to do is get a group of men to go with Sergeant Brown and some to stay here with me to support the mortar crews."

Sergeant Greely pointed to a mortar pit that was about twenty-five feet to our left. He said, "Durham, I want you to get the radio and go to that mortar pit over there and see if you can give them a hand."

I would now take on a new role. Sergeant Greely told the radioman to give me the radio because it would be mine to use. Just about everybody had gotten their assignments. It was midday. I managed to take all my equipment over to the mortar pit I was assigned to. The mortar pit was about fifteen feet in diameter, with sand bags that surrounded it about waist high. I saw the .81-millimeter mortar located right in the middle of the mortar pit. Beyond the perimeter was the huge wood line, which stretched for miles. It surrounded the landing zone from all sides. There was a dead Vietnamese soldier caught up in the concertina wire. He was charcoaled or what you could see that was left of his torso. His effort to get in the perimeter was short-lived. The man was missing body parts, but you could see that it was clearly a body that met its demise. There was no doubt that the Vietcong or NVA was in the area.

Two soldiers were already in the mortar pit. One was black and one was white. The white soldier was a specialist and the other one was a private. The one soldier who was the specialist gave instruction to the private about how to operate the mortar. I was in doubt whether this black soldier had used the mortar before or if he had been trained on the mortar. When I approached the mortar pit, everything stopped. The slightly built specialist with a limp approached me; he was a medium build with brown hair and had somewhat of a Northern accent. He said, "What can I do for you?"

I pulled off the radio and set my M.16 down to the side of the mortar pit. "Sergeant Greely from Echo Company sent me over here to give you a hand." The soldier looked at me briefly and said, "How you doing? My name is Jones. You can just hang loose for a while. I'm trying to tell this private about how to operate this mortar." I then asked him, "Where is the head at? I need to take a leak." The specialist pointed to my rear and said, "The head is right behind headquarters over there."

The huge Eskimo-like bunker was about twelve feet tall and fifty feet wide, filled to the sides and top with sand bags. I picked up my M.16. There was a small road that was plowed on the inside of the perimeter which surrounded the LZ. I wanted to take a little tour on the inside of the perimeter. There was a wooden sign in front of headquarters that said LZ Rita. I looked over in the direction where the dead Vietnamese soldier was in the wire.

The body was in front of a bunker, which had two soldiers with M.60 machine guns who looked out toward the body. All of a sudden, there was a whistling sound—*zzzzzzzzzzzz boom! Boom! Boom!* A loud voice was heard that said, "Incoming! Incoming!" Soldiers started to run and scramble for cover. There were several sporadic explosions going off right behind one another in succession all around me. I was knocked to the ground. My M.16 was separated from me and was blown up by a rocket. In a brief moment, I remembered the incident with Jeff back in the States when I was a little boy.

I remembered when the rifle was dropped into the river while the dogs growled and barked on the shore. I got up off the ground. The only thing that came to mind was to get to the nearest bunker for cover. The nearest bunker was to my left. I ran toward the bunker. The soldiers with the M.60 machine guns started to do their thing as they returned fire. The entrance to the bunker was right in front of me. I began to pick up speed toward the bunker to avoid the explosions that were around me. There were other soldiers that ran toward the bunker I was going to.

There was a soldier in front of me. He decided to dive into the entrance of the bunker as if he were superman while he hit his head on the main plank that held up the bunker. Just as I got in, a round impacted on part of the entrance to the bunker. We made it in just in time. It was not known whether or not this soldier hit his head on purpose or whether or not he was not really thinking about his safety. Inside of the bunker was dark. All of us in the bunker did not speak a word. The soldier who went in head first was in shock as he bled from his head. A round hit into the side of the bunker. The incoming was still present as we saw the flames and smoke go up from the partial entrance of the bunker. One of the soldiers called for a medic. The barrage of incoming was over in a matter of ten minutes or more, and then everything fell silent. A soldier crawled out of the bunker wounded. The medics went into the bunker to attend to the wounded soldier with the head injury. I crawled out the bunker and pissed on the side of the bunker.

The incoming rounds started up again. I began my run back to the mortar pit. I dodged the rounds just in time to escape injury. The incoming rounds came to a stop once again. I finally made it back to the mortar pit. The first thing I heard from the specialist was, "That's how we've been getting hit lately, so we are going to need to get some more mortar rounds to get ready so we won't run out." The specialist pointed to me. "Go down to the helicopter pad, and get some more .81 rounds. They should be in some crates down there. Go get them and bring them to the mortar pit. Don't stay too long because we need those rounds right away." I didn't hesitate. I headed down to the helicopter pad in hopes that there would be no more incoming for a while.

The helicopter pad smoldered from the recent attack. Activity at the helicopter pad started to pick up. I located the crates that I came for. The heads of the .81-millimeter rounds stuck out of the crates. How would I get the crates back to the mortar pit? I looked around. A jeep mule was a little distance away that was not being used. There was a green tarp that was draped over something that was on the jeep. I wanted to remove what was under the tarp so the mule could be used. I moved part of the tarp back when a human hand fell to the side of another body. I continued to pull the tarp back. It was a pile of dead American soldiers under the tarp. Their eyes were all open. The faces with the dead stares looked out in the distance from the bottom to the top.

I looked up at the top of the pile, and it was the head of a body that belonged to a tall white, blond soldier with blue eyes. He was shot between the eyes. I went into shock! It was my first sight of an American shot in such a way. It was a perfect shot. I fell to my knees and wept. *Oh God, please keep me alive! I don't want to die.* I will do everything in my power to get out of here alive. Reality set in. My wits would have to get me out of Vietnam alive. The prayers would begin to come often and frequently for me. It was just that simple. An extraordinary amount of courage would set in. It was the first time that I realized that this was for real.

I was in the presence of at least six soldiers piled up on a cut-off jeep, dead as dead can be. I couldn't help but feel stunned. I snapped back into reality. I got hold of a mule driver to help me load the .81-millimeter crates up on a mule so that we could get them back to the mortar pit. The crates were piled up near the pit to be opened. I opened the crates right away to get the ammo ready. The crates had to be opened with an entrenching tool that I got out of my ruck sack. In between opening boxes of mortars, I would test my radio to see if it worked properly. The squelch was fresh, and I was making contact with headquarters in the compound. The .81 rounds were piled up on the right side of the pit about a good four feet high in layers. There were probably one hundred rounds ready to be put in use. Everything was a little quiet for the moment, and then all hell broke loose. "Incoming! Incoming!" The thuds of the rounds coming into the perimeter made their impacts. Sergeant Greely yelled out, "Man your stations! Man your stations!"

Specialist Jones was the gunner, and the black soldier was the feeder of the .81 mortar. The stakes were set up in alignment. All that was needed now was to know where the enemy fire was coming from. Specialist Jones said to me, "I want you to let me know where the incoming is coming from. So keep your eyes open and let headquarters know." My radio was on along with my M.16. I crouched down in position to peep over the sand bags to see where the enemy was present in the wood line. Specialist Jones said to Private Scott, "I want you to take some charges off those rounds." Private Scott said okay. He got a mortar round and began to take the charges off.

The private who helped Specialist Jones displayed fear in his eyes and gestures. He began to shake. The new black soldier acted like he did not know what was expected of him. All there was to know was we had to return fire and do it without hesitation. Time was of essence to push back this attack. The incoming rounds started to impact more inside the perimeter. The whizzing sound of rounds started to become more apparent. I looked out beyond the perimeter at a vacant spot that seemed to have high jungle weeds about a mile in distance. I could see that this was possibly the area where the rounds were coming from. I got on the radio and called this location into headquarters. Specialist Jones told Private Scott to start putting rounds into the mortar tube. I moved away from the radio to help Private Scott get the rounds. Private Scott started to panic.

Specialist Jones said to Private Scott, "I want you to get the mortar rounds from Private Durham to put in the tube!" A round was given to Private Scott as I waited for him to drop it in the tube. I gave the second round to Private Scott to go in the tube, and before I knew it, Private Scott didn't give the first round time enough to get out of the tube. The second round impacted on the first round, which made Private Scott's fingers collide with the fins of the first round. His fingers were cut off, and the second round never made it in the tube.

The impact caused the first round arched about one hundred feet in the air and impact on a berm along the perimeter about thirty yards away. Specialist Jones and I hit the ground as soon as we saw what happened. The round impacted on the berm and did not go off. Private Scott cried while blood poured from his hand. Specialist Jones called for the medic. Specialist Jones told me, "Come over here, Durham, so we can get these rounds out." I knew what my role was right away, and that was not to make the same mistake Private Scott made.

My role to assist Specialist Jones needed to be done to repel the attack. Private Scott stepped back in extreme pain as he fell down in the mortar pit. With my assistance, we put out about fifty rounds to keep the enemy at bay. Specialist Jones walked the rounds up and down the trail adjacent to the enemy. The rounds were sent out in rapid succession. The enemy started to retreat. The medics came and retrieved Private Scott. The attack soon stopped. I was now a full-fledged mortar-crew member.

Specialist Jones and I handled the mortar in the proper manner. I felt sorry for what had happened to Private Scott. This was something you shouldn't gloat over. My job was to stay focused. Being efficient was important to me. We had to work together as a team. The attack was over, but ammunition still had to be prepared. The medevac helicopters arrived and picked up the wounded.

As I went down to the helicopter pad to get more .81-millimeter rounds, my name was called. "Hey, Durham! I need to talk to you." It was Sergeant Greely. He and First Sergeant Gregory stood outside the mortar pit. I jogged back to the mortar pit. Sergeant Greely approached me along with First Sergeant Gregory who was with him. He was a big mountain of a man, with all his stripes and hash marks from past military campaigns. He was spit-and-polish. His reddish face made him look rugged. He shook my hand and said, "Job well-done, soldier. You will get put in for a commendation medal. I'm impressed about the way you handled yourself." A shiver went up my spine as First Sergeant Gregory gave me this information. "Okay, Sarge, I need to go get some more ammunition."

CHAPTER 7

KEEP THE ENEMY CLOSE

It would be a short while and Echo Company would be on the move again to a different location. All I knew was that my unit was back on reconnaissance, and that was our primary job—to search and destroy. I really didn't want to go out on patrol again. To confront the enemy was hard. Even though our stay was short at LZ Rita, we would be back up on the helicopters again, headed to another destination that was around a province called Tay Ninh, which was rural area near the Ho Chi Minh trail. The trails near Tay Ninh would lead somewhere near enemy locations that was not known by our reconnaissance unit. Our patrol moved along a shallow trail, where we saw a rubber plantation. Our patrol stayed vigilant as we moved through the jungle with precaution and partial heat exhaustion. This area was not remote enough to be away from civilians who would follow close behind us.

Echo Company settled down near a road that was a good quarter of a mile where it was visible. This road was used for commercial travel. You could see the peasants who pedaled goods that would be sold. After being in Vietnam for about two and a half months, this still was not a time to take any chances. By no means would I consider myself as being short. A little of the greenness had worn off. I already had my baptism by fire.

My mind wondered as I looked at the letter that was in my hand. In this letter everything seemed as if we were into a relationship. Some of the soldiers had already received Dear John letters due to the fact that Jody was very much alive back in the States. One day when mail was given out, about five guys received the notorious letter while they opened them in their guarded position in formation. The tears came like drips from a leaky faucet. Guys started to talk about how horny they were and how they missed their wives and children. Sergeant Greely told them about sexually transmitted diseases, which some of the Vietnamese women carried, but he didn't say which type of diseases.

I heard one soldier say he wouldn't fuck any Vietnamese woman because they had razor blades in their pussies. I guess he didn't want to have anything to do with these types of women. Being a married man was not a thing I considered as being because I had not married a woman yet. All I was concerned about was going back to the states alive. Once Echo Company settled in a little bit in our new location, Sergeant Greely announced, "You men are going to need prophylactics if you are going to be dealing with some of these women. I don't want any of you to get the black sif. I asked

Sergeant Greely, "What is the black sif?" Sergeant Greely looked at me and said, "You don't want to know."

All I wanted to know at this time was when it was going to be my turn to experience a woman and what would it be like to have intercourse with her. I wanted to be faithful to Darlene, but I didn't know when I would die.

We got our small shovels out and began to dig into a small perimeter so we could keep an eye on the peasants who were still along the stretch of the highway, which was still visible to us through the woods. The black pajamas along with children and older people seemed to be a friendly group, but we still didn't know if any Vietcong were mixed up in this entourage of peasants, who really looked like they wanted something from the American soldiers. They always wanted to be in our sights.

While I dug my foxhole, I would keep my eyes on the road, where I could see the peasants in front of me or see if there was anything different about them. The little mopeds and motorcycles would drive up and down the road. They would park on the edge of the road with the venders. There were small motorcycles that were attached to carts that had a canopy built on top of it, which was covered by a cloth material. I proceeded to dig my foxhole and get ready for nightfall. Sometimes various soldiers would leave their foxholes to come over and visit to chew the fat and trade c rations, which they preferred instead of the ones they got. Franks and beans were a favorite, along with dark chocolate. The fruit cocktail wasn't too bad, along with a few other items like maybe beef and potatoes, which could appeal to you.

I picked up my M.16 to make sure it was on the ready and close by. This area was not like an LZ, where you could just lay your weapon down and go a few feet in a mortar pit. Nightfall came, and the four-hour or two-hour guard watches were set in motion. No sooner after dusk began, tripflares were illuminated. I got in a prone position in my foxhole so that I could get a fix on my target even though it was dark. The Claymores went off along with the .60s and other small arms. I could hear voices scream. "There's movement o' six hundred! They're trying to get into the perimeter!" *Whssssssssssss bomb! Sizzzzzzzzzz, boom! Boom!* The rpgs and rockets made their presence felt inside our perimeter. I held on to my M.16, pointing outward. I still couldn't see where the enemy fire came from. I turned my head and realized the enemy was trying to breach the rear of our perimeter.

My concentration became immediate in front of me. My trigger finger moved around the trigger. I wanted to keep my position intact. From time to time, I would glimpse to my rear to see what was going on even if it was momentary because I didn't want anybody to sneak up behind me. The soldiers to my rear were involved in the firefight. With the trip flares giving off enough light, I looked to my rear again; I could see some silhouettes, which were the enemy in black pajamas firing off their weapons. Some of them were women. Everything was too close-in to call artillery. The .60 machine guns along with M.16s from Echo Company spewed rounds from their barrels.

The attack would be short-lived. Daylight soon arrived. Sergeant Greely wanted to know if everybody was all right. Sergeant Greely announced that there would be a small patrol going out to see where the attack had come from or see whether or not Echo Company had done any damage. I finished off the cold c rations that I had left. A helicopter came in with supplies. I looked outside the formation to see what would come off the helicopters. All I wanted to see was the red nylon mailbag that would have letters in it.

The moment came when I saw the red mail bag appear from a helicopter, which was being unloaded with other supplies. Supplies of ammunition and hot food were seen being taken off the helicopters by soldiers. A smile came over my face. Sergeant Greely's hand was still bandaged from the previous firefight.

Sergeant Greely told the platoon that the movement of enemy in black pajamas last night was Vietcong women that were found dead along the rear wood line. Sergeant Greely said, "The women helped lead the attack that took place last night. I want you all to be on extra alert because of what had happened last night. Charlie is not going to let us rest. There are also some civilians in this area, so you will have to be on your toes."

I would envy the guys who got mail. It was a joy for the married guys to get mail because they wanted to hear from their wives and family. Being single was a lonely state to be in. To hear from a girl back in the states meant a lot. I would talk to Joe, the big black soldier from Louisiana, about girls. It was just small talk. The mail was being handed out, and Joe was one of the first names called to get his mail. He came over to where my foxhole was to tease me because he had just got mail. He took the envelope and passed it along my nose so that I could get the fragrance of the letter that smelled like some kind of woman's perfume, which was something pleasant.

Joe would jerk the letter away in a quick reaction when I tried to grab it. This would go on for a little while. Now was the time for me to receive some mail. I heard my name called out. "Durham! Here's a letter for you." I climbed out of my foxhole and grabbed my M.16. I walked over to where the mail call was being held. Everyone seemed to be in a relaxed mode, with various weapons dangling or being held close to their person. There was a line for hot meals in metal containers that had just come off the helicopters. Everyone was being served their food from the hot containers. The cooks would be behind the containers to serve the different portions of the meals. The containers were filled up with mostly mashed potatoes, carrots, string beans, bread, and some kind of meat. There was a container of red kool-aid, which looked like blood, along with applesauce.

We would be able to use the paper plates that were present. A longer line was starting to form for chow. I would join the line soon. All I wanted was my one or two letters if I was lucky. It just happened to be one letter as the soldier handed the letter to me. I looked at the letter and saw it was from Charleston, South Carolina. I lifted the letter up to get a whiff. I looked over at Joe and smiled. The difference in this letter is the fact that it wasn't from Darlene but from her sister, Beth. I went to a tree that was nearest to me and got behind it so nobody would see me. I wanted to have some privacy when I read the letter. I scooted down along the edge of the tree while I laid my M.16 down. I turned the safety on. I couldn't help but sniff the letter one more time.

I felt odd when I opened the letter. Why was Darlene's sister writing me? I pealed the letter open. The letter started off

Dear Carroll,

This is Beth, and I hope everything is fine with you. I know it is a bad time to write a letter like this to you, but it is something that Darlene didn't want to do, so I decided to write the letter for her to stop her from feeling bad about it. Darlene has found somebody new. She said that she was in love with this person and she wanted him to be her new boy friend. She wants to move and go live with him until they get married.

I'm sorry it won't be able to work out between you and her. I felt that she needed to tell you this, but I'm doing it instead.

At that moment, a knife seemed as if it had pierced my heart. I never felt that way before. I never thought I would experience something like this in the jungles of Vietnam. At this particular moment, I didn't want to continue to read the letter. The thrill was gone. I folded up the letter to pretend that nothing had happened and put it in my pocket to discard it at a convenient time. I was devastated as tears came to my eyes. After I ate, I went back to my foxhole perimeter position. I felt like I was hit by a ten-ton truck.

I couldn't help but see the activity that was in front of him. The peasants were pedaling their wares. All of a sudden, I noticed a young Vietnamese woman who caught my attention. She had on one of those straw hats that most of the women would wear. Her oval face was distinct, along with her slanted eyes and small figure, which pleased me. Her black pajamas and sandals stood out. She also had on the white blouse to match her Vietnamese outfit. She paced back and forth in front of one of those made-up carts that were present. She looked over at me. I was no more than two hundred yards away from this woman. I became intrigued by this woman even though I had just got my heart broken from a letter that I had got not too long ago.

She waved a handkerchief at me along with a smile on her face. She seemed like she wanted my company. I took this as an invitation for me to meet her. I looked back into the perimeter to see what was going on within the unit. I thought the cart the woman stood around would give me some cover so I wouldn't be seen. My response was to get over to where she was.

All I knew was that I had to make a move and do it undetected along with my M.16 and additional ammo. The helicopters move in and out with ammunition along with other supplies. Soldiers stood in the chow line. I felt this was a live-or-die situation. I also wondered if I would ever get to experience a woman at the age of nineteen. The chance had to be taken. I made sure once again that my M.16 was full with a twenty-round clip in it along with it being on automatic.

I looked once again around the perimeter to see where Sergeant Greely was or any other platoon leader. I saw the way was clear and made my move. I grabbed my M.16 and jumped up out of my foxhole with stealth and ran over to where the woman was. I decided to throw caution to the wind but still be aware of what I was doing without looking back. I was soon in the little cart after the woman had gone in before me. It was a small space, but there was room enough for both of us. I noticed that there was a medium-sized chest or what appeared to be a cooler that contained beer and wine covered in rice hulls. The water looked cold along with the beer. I looked at the labels on the bottles that stood in the cooler. I gripped my M.16 and lifted the bottles up and examined them. It was rice wine and what they called tiger beer. I had no plans to get intoxicated.

The first thing the woman said, "You number 1 GI or you number 10?" I said "I'm number 1 GI" with a smile on my face. A warm feeling came over me as I looked at the woman. I kept my eye on the old man who appeared to be the driver of the vehicle. The *papasan* turned around and looked at me with my M.16 in my hand. I aimed the weapon at the old man and said, "You keep looking ahead and mind your business." The papasan turned his head in a quick fashion to the front. The Asian woman captivated me. I knew at this time that I was in the presence of my enemies.

I would not hesitate to kill any of these people in my presence while I held my M.16 in the ready position in case any wrong moves were made. I clutched my M.16 with a purpose to not let it go. I had my head on a pivot as I gazed at the woman along with the surroundings. I was in complete control because I had the weapon. I inspected the inside of the vehicle with my M.16.

My peripheral vision was on cue because I didn't want anything to get pass me. A rat jumped out of the cart all of a sudden. There were little bowls of rice and bamboo shoots that were used for meals. I was not there to have lunch. My interest was on the woman I had just met. She pointed to the items in the small space and gestured with her hands as she spoke broken English. She said, "You see? You want beer? You want wine, GI?" I had become restless; I didn't want to stay in the covered cart too much longer. I said, "You speak English?" I motioned to the female and said, while pointing the M.16 to her private parts between her legs, "You have boom boom." This was the language that meant pussy. The young woman looked at me and smiled. She said, "You have money?" I had some money from being paid in the field, which was five dollars.

I began to get aroused. My penis got hard. The Vietnamese woman looked at me and began to touch my bulging penis from the imprint of my fatigues pants. I reached in my pants pocket and pulled out a five dollar bill. The papasan pretended to look at me once again. The M.16 was still in my grasp, aimed at him and the woman. I handed the money to the woman. She grabbed my hand and pulled me to come with her. She climbed out of the cart. I peeked out of the structure to see if the way was clear. I looked over to where my unit was to make sure that they were still there and to see if anyone had missed me.

The way was clear. I followed the woman into the woods. We sneaked our way to an area that was sparsely wooded but out of the way. I looked up and down the trail with caution. We were out of sight away from where we had just come from. I kept my head on a constant pivot. I then asked her, "How old are you?" She said with a sly smile, "Me twenty-three. I believe you beaucoup butterfly." I thought to myself, was she really twenty-three? How would I know? Maybe she was only nineteen? She was a woman and that was all that counted. She looked down at my fatigue pants where the imprint of my penis was still bulging out. She felt it. We went to a small open area. We stopped, and she got on her knees in front of me. I held my M.16 in one hand while she unbuttoned my pants. I looked up and down the trail to see if I had been detected by the enemy.

I looked into the exotic woman's eyes. She pulled her straw hat off and proceeded to pull down the black pajamas that went below her navel. I looked down in her vagina area, where her pubic hairs could be seen that surrounded her pussy. Euphoria came over me. She pulled my fatigues pants down and touched my penis. She pulled me down to the ground and guided my penis into her vagina.

I began to stroke the woman. My virginity had been broken in the remote jungle of Vietnam, seven thousand miles away from home. The excitement made me feel a joyous triumph just after I received the Dear John letter from the states. I continued to stroke her as we laughed. Through all the excitement, I didn't let my guard down. The pussy was enjoyed while my head was on a pivot. The grip on my M.16 made it go into the dirt. The Vietnamese woman smiled while she looked up at me.

The woman would look over at my weapon to see if it was still in my possession. My trigger finger caressed the trigger on the M.16 ever so gentle. I climaxed, and it was all over. While on my knees, I got up off the ground and pulled up my pants while I still held on to my weapon. The area was clear, and there were no surprises. I would have to get back to Echo Company right away. The woman proceeded to pull up her black pajamas. I would repeat this covert activity with this woman for several days. There was no passionate kiss because I knew this could not last. There still were attempts for me and Leea to communicate, but it was understood that we would see each other again. She said to me again, "You beaucoup butterfly?" I looked at her once again and smiled. She felt my cock. "You number 1. You good fuck."

To get back to Echo Company was still a matter of stealth. The escapade had gone undetected. Our rendezvous began to take on a different meaning for me. There developed a love between both of us. The added risk was still there and also the danger because no one knew about this love affair but Leea and I along with the papasan. I had fallen in love with Leea. The sex was unprotected, but it was something that I had to experience.

I would go out to meet her when I was sure the way was clear. Perhaps some of the other soldiers did the same thing, but this was something that I wanted to keep a secret. I did not think about the trouble I could have gotten into. Our sexual act would not be in the same location because I knew it would be dangerous to give away my position. The enemy was always taken into consideration.

I took a picture of me out of my wallet, which was taken of me in high school, to show Leea. It was my graduation picture in my cap and gown. This was a moment when I told Leea what it was like in America. I said, "The United States is a beautiful country." I also had another picture of me in uniform as I stood near a house back in the States. I showed the picture to Leea with a great amount of delight. I said, "You see this picture? This is me at home in the

United States." She looked up at me and at the picture while she smiled with her big black eyes. She pulled her wide straw hat off. I was once again excited as she groped for my penis so that we could begin our act. I gave her my graduation picture of me in my cap and gown. I said to her, "Here, you can have this one."

There was a beam that came over her face that made this seem like it was important to her. Leea had a few pictures of her own. She pulled the pictures out from her person. One picture of her looked like it was made in some kind of picture studio. One was of her as she sat in a straw chair with an arched back along with her straw hat on. She looked like a queen. She also had a picture of herself with just a head shot without a hat on and her hair in a long flowing style with a pretty smile on her face. I touched her face as my fingers moved along her nose and lips. My M.16 was still firm in my hand as I looked around with my normal vigilance to make sure we weren't being watched.

I kissed and groped her with one hand while I pulled down her pants. I wanted to enjoy every minute of this engagement because there was not that much time left as I looked back up the trail. The excitement of the sexual act exhilarated me. The quickies were something to look forward to each day that Echo Company would stay in the area. The friendship that grew between me and Leea was unbelievable. This foreign woman who was my enemy was someone I fell in love with. This was a booty call in the jungles of Vietnam. One day, I handed Leea another five dollar bill. She pushed my hand away. She refused to take the money at this point. It came as a surprise to me. She had fallen in love with me. The two or three weeks would seem like months to me as time went by. My adventure and fear did not keep me away from this woman. When I saw Leea, it gave me comfort while I had to face my other enemy. If the enemy knew of me, I would just have to face him.

I was superior to this woman whom I fell in love with. The meetings took on a relationship that couldn't be denied. To kill this woman was not beyond me if she betrayed me in any manner that would threaten my life. The idea of me letting my guard down was not in my conscious.

One day, I handed Leea another five dollar bill. She pushed my hand away. She refused to take the money while we sat in the makeshift cart. At this point, the relationship had gotten much stronger. The word had come down for Echo Company to move on. It would be in the matter of a few days. When I told Leea about the move, it broke her heart. Just before the unit's departure, I attempted to see her one more time.

My ability to see her one more time would be my last. I tried to ask the papasan where she was. He just looked at me in an odd way. In vain, I tried to make the papasan understand what it was I wanted. I even shook him and said, "Where is Leea?" I decided to look in some of the places where we had made love. Maybe she was already with someone else. My search was to no avail. There was one final area that I went to. It had no comfort for me. There lay on the ground in pieces was one of the pictures that I had given her. I picked up the little pieces of the picture to attempt to put it back together. My heart sank once again. While I looked around the area, a butterfly flew from off a bush.

CHAPTER 8

EXISTING ON THE EDGE

The romantic episode came to an end. I decided to continue, and the soldier was on because our unit was due to go back on out to do some reconnaissance, which I really didn't look forward to. The energy to move on was one of anguish as the unit saddled up that next morning to go to another location that would be hostile. The helicopters came in to pick us up to a new location, which was kept secret. I took one more look back at the peddler's carts to see where the rendezvous started between me and Leea. There was no Leea. The helicopters warmed up so that we could get on our way. Sergeant Greely told us that we would be going to an undisclosed location somewhere in the delta. I was at a loss because this new mission was on my mind. The National Vietnamese Army was on my mind because they were more hardcore than the Viet Cong.

This time up in the helicopter, everything was different as far as the landscape was concerned. The greenery seemed like it stood out more as the forest presented a pattern that seemed ideal for the enemy to hide. The rice paddies and fields took on the rural look. There were cement houses that started to appear in the landscape. They were many miles apart from one another. The remoteness then became obvious. The gear that I carried mattered a lot to me as I inspected it and felt the tightness of the backpack and web gear while I held my M.16. The hot air in my face made my cross around my neck twist and turn.

The helicopters began to find their location as they set down. I saw Sergeant Greely depart the lead helicopter that he was in, along with the first sergeant. They jumped from the helicopter into the elephant grass. Sergeant Greely started motioning for us to move out of our helicopters. Echo Company began to descend from the helicopters. Everything was still out in the open and exposed until we would get into the tree line that was about two hundred yards away. In quick time, we would get to the clump of trees as soon as possible.

We soon got into formation in the proper position. I could see Smitty up near Sergeant Greely, who was in the point man position. The .60 machine gun man came into vision. He was in his regular position, about three to four men back. I looked back and could see the First Cav symbol on the helicopters. They soon departed.

There also was another machine gunner who carried the .60; his name was Carlos. He was Mexican. Carlos had volunteered to carry the .60. He kept asking Sergeant Greely to get him a .60 while we were at our previous location. He finally got his wish. The unit still needed much more fire power; I knew that big Joe wasn't giving up his .60. I always liked being light so I could carry my M.16 with ease on rock and roll because I still had plenty of fire power for now. I still had three bandoliers along with my taped-up magazines inside my M.16.

Carlos was just a little lighter in weight than me, but I still felt that I was the stronger. I knew that strength could be measured and felt I was good enough to confront any man in my unit. If anyone wanted to try me, I wouldn't mind the challenge no matter how big you were. Even though Carlos could handle the .60, it made no difference to me. Carlo's hair would dangle in his eyes when he wasn't wearing his red bandana. Carlos was kind of scrawny but cocky. He seemed to like the idea of going out on patrol to look for VC. He was also kind of skittish. His complexion was dark like the Mexicans, so he stood out. He also seemed to be a jokester. He wasn't really that gung ho but just a little bit. He certainly wasn't as gung ho as Sergeant Greely; no one in the unit was as gung ho as the old feisty World War II veteran. But Carlos was always ready for some action.

So far the new area posed no threat. I kept my eyes peeled as I looked up and down the tree line at every tree I thought a Vietcong might be in. A dream came to me one night. A Vietcong was well camouflaged up in a tree He aimed his AK-47 at me. He looked through his scope and got me in his cross hairs. He moved the aim from my crouch to my head. I soon woke up in my prone position as I lay on top of my M.16.

It was good to get under some shade from the heat, which made you feel like you were uptight, which was the case for me. The word had come from Sergeant Greely that Echo Company would hump about five more clicks for the day. I rechecked my gear to make sure everything was still in order. I was in my regular position in formation near the radio man, which was still a vulnerable position.

The previous radio man had gone home. His time was up, and he departed while our unit was at our last encampment. New guys continued to rotate in and out of the unit.

It was hard for me to know some of the soldiers who were short, and their time was getting closer to going home. This particular march was long and arduous because of the heat and the soreness of my feet, which seemed to ache with every step on the terrain of Vietnam. The sun light showed in between the canopy and the wooded area that presented itself all around the unit. Smitty hacked his way through the rough jungle patches of tall elephant grass as he walked point. Sergeant Greely said, "All right, men, it's time to take a break!"

I heard Smitty complain again about walking point. Smitty would move back into the unit after being out in the front. He complained about the dangerous point position. His eyes seemed glazed as Smitty spoke. "I'm fucking tired of walking point! This machete is in my way! I'm ready to kill some VC! It's time for somebody else to take point. I'm too damn short!" Smitty leaned up against a tree as he pulled his kool pack of cigarettes out of his fatigue pocket. He continued to speak. "My feet are tired, and so are my arms!

"How much longer are we going to be out here in these sticks? Every day it's the same old shit. Why do I have to walk point when there are plenty other guys out here who can do the job." Sergeant Greely answered Smitty, "Right now, Smitty, you've got the most time walking point, and that is one of the main reasons that I have you up there in that position whether you like it or not. Smitty, you know we need to know where Charlie is, so stop crying and just do your job." The glaze in Smitty's eyes seemed to sharpen as he looked at Sergeant Greely. Smitty said with no trepidation in his voice,

"You must think I'm crazy, don't you think that people get tired of walking point all the time?! Sarge, I'm getting too short for this shit! I just want to go home!" Sergeant Greely replied, "Someday we're all going to go home, but for right now, we have some business to take care of, so get your act together!"

As Sergeant Greely returned the glare, he got up close to Smitty and looked down at him and said, "I don't know where you are going with this, soldier, but I know one thing, and that is you have a fuckin' job to do, and if it's walking point, then that is what you're going to do! Do you understand that?" Smitty just stared at Sergeant Greely, who seemed like he was on his last nerve as he stared Smitty down. Smitty backed off. He turned around and walked back to the point position. He stomped his feet in disgust. "Fuck this shit! I'll be glad when I get the fuck out of here."

Everyone stood in silence while the argument had taken place. I yelled to Smitty, "Hey, Smitty, give me a smoke?" Smitty turned and looked at me and threw a pack of kools back at me and said, "Who do the fuck you think I am? Here you go again, humming and bumming like a B-52." We both smiled at each other as I caught the pack of smokes.

As soon as I got a cigarette out of the pack, I threw the pack back to Smitty. There was one more look of disgust from Smitty as he stared at Sergeant Greely and proceeded to go back to his unwanted position in the field. The soldier named Harry walked up with his fitted boonie cap on and got into the conversation. He had a mischievous look on his face. He walked toward Smitty. His remark to Smitty was, "That's right, shorty. You tell 'um. This fucking shit is getting old! We getting too short for this shit!" Harry stood not too far from where I stood. Sergeant Greely turned to him and said, "Soldier, the same thing goes for you! You might think this is a joke, but we all have a job to do, and we are going to do it if it means taking other measures that I'm sure you wouldn't like." A sneer came on Harry's face as he stared at Sergeant Greely. Harry did an about-face as he turned around to go back to his position.

He said to himself, "I'd like to catch that motherfucker in Watts when we get home, I'd bust him in his head." Sergeant Greely wasn't finished; he said, "We are all tired, but we are going to get through this!" The conversation had ceased while some soldiers opened their canteens to get their thirst quenched from the heat.

Sergeant Greely retorted, "I want everybody to stay alert because we're going to be moving out shortly." He said, "Durham, I want you to take up the rear for now, so go and get in your position, but before you go back to the rear, me and Top would like to have a word with you." I wondered about what Sergeant Greely wanted to say to me. He also called Joe over to join in on the conversation. I hoped this conversation wouldn't be like the one he had between Smitty and Harry. Everyone was trying to extinguish their cigarettes or finish their snacks from the c rations they had opened up. Joe and I came over to where we would meet with Sergeant Greely and First Sergeant Gregory. Sergeant Gregory always seemed to be an imposing figure as he stood next to Sergeant Greely. His experience as a soldier seemed to stand out, which I noticed back at LZ Rita. I looked up to him as a mentor. I would hang on to his every word.

Sergeant Greely was the one who spoke. "Top, don't you have something to tell these men?" I knew First Sergeant Gregory had the most experience because of his rank. Joe grinned as he stood with the. 60 machine gun positioned over shoulder. He carried it proudly. The first sergeant said, "We have observed you men, and we feel that you all would be good candidates for leadership school.

You're already specialists. We need some more leadership, this will give you all a chance to make sergeant. So you'll be getting orders shortly so you can attend that school. So in the meantime, continue to do your jobs and work as a team so that we can go home." First Sergeant Gregory said, "I want to go back to those hills of Georgia and see ma ma so that I can have some peace. We'll let you know when y'all be going. You can go back to your positions because we got some ground to cover today."

We didn't want to disappoint our enemy. Joe and I returned to where we were assigned as if nothing happened. It was hard for me to imagine a leadership school in the middle of Vietnam. What ever it took to be a good soldier and get home safe meant a lot to me. Sergeant Greely made the call. "All right, men, let's saddle up!" With slow movement, the soldiers started to pick up backpacks while some grabbed their M.16s and other weapons. There was always reluctance in the air when those two words were said. One soldier said, "Oh, do we have to?" It was like a shiver went up your spine, or you could see that look in the eyes of the soldiers that told you something was about to happen. This day would drag on as the unit stayed in a line formation. Every other soldier would have their weapons pointed out in the direction of the enemy. Everybody would cover one another's back as much as possible.

This particular trail wound around bends. You would never know what was behind that bend. A good ten clicks had already been walked when Sergeant Greely announced that it was time to take a break. Sergeant Greely said, "All right, men, I want you to spread out a little bit apart so that you won't get in each other's way. We'll be here for a little while until we get our bearings straight so we know where the fuck where're going." I found a big tree with a large root that was on the side of the tree to give me some cover. I would not relax and take off my back pack because I felt we would mount up in another ten minutes.

I sat down against the back of the tree. I would be able to look around the tree to see the soldier that was in front of me. This had been a long patrol. It was quiet, and there were no birds or other animals making noises. The sun shone bright along with pockets of light, which hypnotized me as I sat under the shade of the trees. I held my M.16 upright as I leaned against the tree. My eyes began to close as I nodded into a nap, which I had no intention of doing. My M.16 was clutched in my hand.

I didn't know how long it was that I was asleep. Red ants began to crawl on me. They moved onto my skin in a brisk manner. The stings felt like bee stings as they made their presence known around my neck and farther down my back. I brushed my hand in pain across my neck. The stinging sensation was made worse by the sweat that accumulated on my back. I squirmed in pain. I got up quickly from my position. I wanted to remove my ruck sack but decided to take my fatigue shirt tail out so the ants would fall down onto the ground as I jumped in disgust.

The stings continued until the ants began to fall to the ground. I began to stomp the ants with my boots. I looked around the tree to see if the soldier that was in front of me was still there. To my surprise, no one was there. The unit had moved on and left me behind. Panic set in because now I felt that I was all alone and vulnerable. I knew at this point that I must be in control. I gathered my composure. I knew that my unit was headed north. My stealth movement became present as I walked slow and looked around as if I were hunting for prey. A snake dangled from a tree right in front of me. I took aim and did not squeeze the trigger. The snake showed its fangs. I turned my M.16 into a baseball bat. The butt of my M.16 took the snake's head off.

My sense of where the unit had gone started to become more conscious. The mistake had been made, but now was not the time to linger on it. I looked around to my rear to see if anyone was behind me. I knew that my focus had to be concentrated in front of me. There was another bend that was ahead in the trail as I looked at the emptiness of the jungle ahead. I had no idea how much time had gone by. I made my way to the mouth of the bend. I looked to the left. I could see that my unit was not far away. It was a great relief to see my unit not far away.

The soldier in front of me didn't even know I had been lost. I was glad that he didn't recognize that I was gone because he could have been one of those soldiers who were trigger-happy. He should have known that I was behind him. This was one mistake that I would never make again. I noticed a small gathering of soldiers in my unit off to the side of the trail. I went over to where the soldiers were gathered. I pushed a couple of soldiers to the side so I could see what they were looking at. They stood over a dead NVA. The body was bloated but not fully decomposed; the soldier was lying on his side. He had on a grayish type of uniform bottom.

Sergeant Greely was with the group of soldiers. Sergeant Greely leaned down and rolled the body on its back. The dead Vietnamese soldier was short in stature. He had his black sandals still on. His face had turned a grayish brown. The NVA soldier had been mutilated; his penis had been sewn in his mouth by a needle and thread. A First Cav patch was sewn on his chest. His eyes were wide open. He had a gaping hole in his chest below the patch.

A death stare was in this soldier's eyes. It was simply the case of overkill, which shouldn't have happened. Sergeant Greely responded to the men, "Now this is the type of thing that we don't want to be a part of because all it does is make us look bad." One of the soldiers shouted out, "Fuck that motherfucker!" Sergeant Greely then said, "All right, men, let's break it up! Let's go! Get back in formation! We still have some more ground to cover before nightfall." This enemy soldier would have a burial if one of his own kind had found him. He must have gotten separated from his unit. The hardness of war started to take its grip on me. The journey continued on as I thought about what we had just seen. What would possess a man to mutilate another human being as if he were some kind of animal? The overkill of war was something I didn't want to subject myself to because I felt that it was enough just to kill a man. I wanted to make sure that I kept my composure as much as possible in order for me to be able to control the enemy on my own terms.

A scent was in the air; we made our way through the jungle. There was moisture in the air. The smell was the smell of rain. The first partial down pour presented itself in an unexpected manner. The poncho that I had in my ruck sack would be of some use, but the thought came about how you would keep your weapon dry so that it would be able to fire.

Sergeant Greely and the first sergeant found a location not too far from a wood line that looked like a place to set up a perimeter for the night.

Sergeant Greely announced, "Okay, men, it's time to set up a perimeter! So let's get started so that we can have our outposts put out. We have to dig in, so let's get started." The rain started to pour. Time was of essence because it started to get dark. I located my entrenching tool, which was attached in my ruck sack. I started the process to dig my foxhole The ground was soft and mushy, but it wasn't quite as soft about a good two feet down. I tried to look out through and past the elephant grass, which appeared like several large football fields. The idea of not knowing what was out there was always a mystery. To the sides of the fields were additional wood lines.

The sun disappeared into the wood line. Then the rain came again to fill up my partially made foxhole. The darkness made more of its appearance. All I could do was go by feeling my way as I dug the fox hole. I glanced to my sides to see what the other soldiers were doing. From what I could see, none of them had a complete foxhole dug. I began to cover myself with my poncho. The rain started to soak through my poncho. I strapped my M.16 over my shoulder to point the weapon down so the inside of the barrel would not get wet. The shallow foxhole I dug was halfway filled up with water. The foxhole soon turned to mud. I grew tired from the ordeal with this new element that I had to confront along with the rest of the troops.

There was no sleep to be gotten this night because of the conditions that were not conducive to any human being who didn't have the proper shelter because of the fact that you were rained on and there was nothing you could do about it. All you could do was pray that this misery would stop. I lay down in a prone position on the edge of the foxhole covered by my poncho with my head sticking out while my M.16 did the same thing. My eyes tried to shut for sleep, but at the same time, my mind and body were holding off with an effort to get through this ordeal. With little sleep, day light seemed so far away. The muddiness sunk in on the front of my fatigues. The few stars in the sky seemed so distant. Small torrents of rain would come off and on.

Soon daylight arrived once again. I woke to regroup in a mode of restlessness and dampness. I managed to locate a few c rations. The fruit cocktail and crackers would serve as breakfast on this damp morning along with water from my canteen. This would hold me until we were able to get something warm to eat. The helicopters were expected to come in with supplies for the day. I searched for my toothbrush and toothpaste. I knew they were somewhere in my rucksack as I searched. Some mud had managed to get in the area where I found the dental items. All the men inspected their equipment to wipe off some of the mud. They wanted to see what was dry. The ammo was checked to see if it was dry. The poncho liners served their purpose because some of the areas on the liners were dry. You could use the dry part as a cloth. The sun would also do its job to keep equipment dry.

As Echo Company got near the haunted wood line, Sergeant Greely made an announcement. "All right, men, listen up." Everyone in Echo Company came to a halt. "We're going to a little firebase a little ways north of here. We're going to give them reinforcements to help them out for a little while. We will also do some patrolling in the area. I know a lot of you don't like to patrol, so that is some of what we're going to be doing. So don't get your hopes up because this won't be a stand-down, so be ready.

"From what I hear, Charlie is going to be active in the area. The helos will meet up with us so that we can get to this base camp." I hoped that this base camp would be kind of big like LZ Rita was. From the description that Sergeant Greely gave, this firebase wasn't going to be as big as LZ Rita. Sergeant Greely said, "Maybe we'll be able to get a hot meal. Don't get your hopes up because we will make some contact with the enemy. There will also be some individual assignments once we get there. There will also be some outpost in the area that we will have to relieve. Let's move out so we can get the hell out of here! I don't like the idea of being near this wood line, so let's get moving."

CHAPTER 9

DEEP IN THE BOONIES

It was right before dusk when we landed on the new firebase. It seemed like it was small enough to accommodate a few companies and a mortar platoon. The area seemed closed in, but there was enough room to have outposts and small artillery pieces. As soon as Echo Company formed up, assignments were given out by Sergeant Greely near a set-up mortar pit, which was about a hundred yards from where the shitters were located. The men stood around Sergeant Greely, listening for further instructions. The first thing Sergeant Greely said as we stood among the armaments was, "All right, men, I want you to listen and listen carefully because I don't know how long we are going to be here, so pay close attention because your life may depend on it.

"I know we've been out here a little while, but this is something that came from the top. The reason we are here is for support until these guys get set up. First of all, I'd like to say so far so good. That means so far, men, we have no casualties, and I'd like to keep it that way other than the little scrapes and bruises. So thank your lucky stars it's been no more than that. Now let's get down to business. I have assignments to give out! Some of you men will be going on night patrol.

"So what you'll have to depend on is the moon. I know some of you have flashlights, but the main thing is not to give away your position because Charlie will be waiting. So I'll call your name out so that you and your platoon leader can be on your way." The sun had begun to set. On this particular night, I would not be called to go on night patrol, which was a relief to me. Sergeant Greely turned around and pointed to the mortar pit. "Durham, I'm assigning you to this mortar pit." The mortar pit appeared to be in decent shape because somebody had been there before. The .81-millimeter mortar was in the middle of the mortar pit with the small fortified hooch attached to it. Some sand bags supported the little tin roof of the hooch. The sand bags would give you a little protection. A scrawny specialist appeared from the hooch. His fatigues were torn and dirty. His hair was brown, along with his pale complexion. His boots were worn down to the soles.

Sergeant Greely turned and looked over at the specialist and said, "Specialist Jeff Hornby is going to be in charge of this pit, so, Durham, I want you to listen to him because he knows how to operate the mortar. This is your squad leader for now." Sergeant Greely asked Jeff, "How many days have you been here, Jeff?"

"I've been here a little while, but I'm starting to get short."

"You know what you have to do, Specialist Hornby. So I'm going to leave Durham with you so he can get more familiarity with the mortar. So I'll see you all later." I set my gear to the side while I looked at the mortar pit. There were some old stakes up about one hundred yards out. I walked over to the mortar and looked down into the scope, where I could see that the hair lines were aligned up with the distance of the stakes in comparison to the wood line. I could see the wood line where potential enemy targets could be.

The .81-millimeter rounds were staked along the right side of the mortar pit about three feet high and six feet in length. There appeared to be more than one hundred .81-millimeter rounds to our disposal. Mainly, this was a two-man operation with me and Jeff at the helm. Jeff said to me, "I want you to be the feeder, and I'll be the gunner. We will alternate on guard duty so we can get some sleep." I was ready to engage the enemy as my confidence began to grow some more. Specialist Hornby and I would walk the pit as the night went on. I observed the soldier that was superior to me in our squad relationship because I knew that it was important for us to be in sync together. We had to depend on each other.

It was like a game between me and the enemy. It was a matter of who would be caught off guard. Jeff did not say much. I was quiet but felt like there was an appropriate time to talk to your squad leader. Jeff carried a knife, which looked similar to a bowie knife. He had a piece of wood that he would carve on. I nodded off and on while I sat on an ammo box with my M.16 laid across my lap for assurance. I asked Jeff, "How long you been in country?" Jeff answered in a terse manner. "I've been here a little over six months."

"You like it here?"

"What do the fuck you think?!"

"I hear you, man! This place is starting to become like waiting for hell to break loose. My company is not going to be here that long. We were supposed to get about six new replacements. They haven't showed up yet. A lot of guys around here are gung ho and don't give a damn.

"The gooks have been active around here. So everybody here is touchy. I get sick and tired of hearing all the fucking rumors around here, plus I'm getting ready to go on R & R. I don't want anything to interfere with that." Jeff groped his crotch area and said, "I'm gonna get some boom boom. You know what I mean." I said, "Yeah!"

"I should hear something pretty soon. Top told me that it should be any day now. I put in for it a few days ago."

"I'll probably put in for my R & R in a few more months. I'd like to get it close to my date of departure. I just don't want to go home in a body bag." Jeff said, "I'm waiting for a care package that I should be getting from home any day now. My mom told me that she would send one to me every two months or so. Sometimes it takes a long time to get those packages. It depends a lot of times on how slow those guys are back at home and in the rear."

Daylight made its presence once again. I still had not gotten a hot meal in several days or a change of clean fatigues in some weeks as I came out of the hooch. I wiped across my eyes. The c rations had gotten down to the undesirables. I noticed that Jeff had gotten a little more unsettled. He threw his knife down into the dirt as he sat in the corner of the mortar pit on a pallet. He said to me, "We have a few things we need to get done today."

He pointed at the man-made shitters in the back of our hooch. "I want you to go over there where those shitters are and get some diesel fuel so that some of that shit can be burned. I know that it smells awful, but it has to be done. Believe me, I've burned enough shit since I've been here, and it stinks. So don't forget to take your weapon. It won't take you that long to do it." The engineers seemed like they had done a good job building the stalls, which had about six open seats where you could do your business.

There was one main door on it, along with a roof on top and a platform where your feet would rest along with a back wall. Underneath was where all the cut out diesel barrels were placed under the seats on a movable plywood that could be moved out so that you could pour the diesel fuel in to light it. The diesel fuel was in containers that would be used to fuel vehicles that were used on the firebase.

I pulled out three barrels and lit them, waiting for the mess to ignite. When I lit the fuel, it made a billowy gray smoke that seeped through the camp. Human feces and piss would make me fan the smoke to clear my nostrils. Then all of a sudden, the commotion started: "Incoming! Incoming! Incoming!" The whistle and explosions of rounds dug up the earth. I dropped everything and picked up my M.16 and made a breakaway run toward the mortar pit. The incoming rounds hit all around me as I made my way back to the mortar pit. The incoming rounds of mortar and rockets impacted inside the firebase. I jumped in the mortar pit and noticed that Jeff wasn't in the pit. I yelled out, "Jeff! Jeff! Jeff! We got incoming!"

Jeff emerged from the hooch. He seemed as if he were in kind of a haze and was just waking up. With all the commotion that went on, it would seem that he would have been out in the pit even before I had gotten there. He then told me, "I want you to get on the gun! I need to get some of these rounds ready." Jeff went over to where the mortar rounds were. I set my M.16 down and did what Jeff asked me to do. I propped up the mortar on its tripods and glanced out toward the flashes that I glimpsed in the wood-line area that was out in front of me about a mile out. I could see some of the incoming rounds land on the western side of the perimeter. I looked into the sights of the mortar. The stakes were in the proper position to shoot the mortars in that direction. I noticed a soldier on a bunker with a machine gun sitting up on it, directing fire in the same area.

While Jeff pulled some of the charges off the rounds, he told me, "That's right, aim it in that direction, and I'll be over there in a second." I propped the tripod up again toward my targets. I turned the barrel down so that I would get some distance down range to get the rounds on top of the enemy. I adjusted the mortar once again. I yelled over to Jeff, "I need those rounds! It seemed as if Jeff had come out of his daze as the incoming rounds seemed like they were getting closer.

The enemy's mortars walked in as they made their adjustments. I looked at Jeff and said, "Hurry up with those rounds!" Soon I started to receive rounds to go into the mortar tube. It was a matter of a few seconds, and the rounds were going out. I stood over the mortar tube as Jeff gave me the rounds to go out with an extreme amount of coordination. I continued to look into the sight to make sure I was on target.

The out going rounds countered the enemy's fire. Our artillery rounds' going out started to make their presence known. The outgoing mortar rounds had to be continuous to keep counter fire on the enemy. While the enemy's rounds were subsiding, they were on the run because of our counter fire. Jeff and I were relentless. We did not let up. We began to take turns to relieve each other from the mortar. It was important that we were in sync. A third man would have been some relief, but it wasn't time to worry about that now.

We had to use our ingenuity to get through the attack with fierce determination because the base of fire power must be kept intact. It must be at a better pace than the enemy because you did not want to give him an edge.

The insurgents were on the run while some of their men dropped because of the rounds that dropped near them and on them. We had to have a good sense of where they were in order to repel their attack because they were on foot and would not stay in one place very long. The enemy moved around with quickness as they would continue to use small mortars, rockets, and RPGs as some hid and used camouflage.

They wanted to do their damage and leave without any counter fire, but that did not happen. Their effort was thwarted, and that was the way it went as far as we were concerned. We fought them for about half an hour. It wouldn't be long until we had to replenish our ammunition as our number of rounds dwindled. About half of the .81-millimeter rounds had been used. The shitters were destroyed. Several of our soldiers were wounded as we saw medics scramble over to the area near where the shitters were.

We were worn out because of this ordeal. The battle came to a cease. All we wanted to do now was get some rest. Jeff seemed to take everything in stride, but I really didn't know how he felt inside. Jeff and I would take turns to go down on the helicopter pad to pick up ammunition to hump on our shoulders back to the mortar pit. We had not seen Sergeant Greely or Top, but we knew they were somewhere around. Hopefully, the patrols that went out didn't make any contact or get caught up in a cross fire or ambush. Sergeant Greely appeared on the eastern part of the firebase. The patrol he was in appeared to be intact. Even though I still thought Sergeant Greely was still a little gung ho, I was glad to see him and

Top. Smoldering debris lay around as the patrol made their way back inside the perimeter.

I thought this was a good time to get some shut-eye while most of the company seemed to be back from the field. I noticed that Sergeant Greely had come back with a Vietnamese scout. This soldier seemed to be well dressed and small in stature. He had on camouflaged battle fatigues. He was a couple of inches shorter than Sergeant Greely. He carried an M.16 with a few bandoliers. His bush hat made him look the very part of a kit carson scout. I had never seen a Vietnamese scout before or a Vietnamese soldier who was supposed to be an ally for us Americans. Did he give the United States the best intelligence? It seemed like Sergeant Greely and First Sergeant Gregory admired the soldier as they talked in Vietnamese and English.

Guard duty was tedious for me that night. The recovery from the battle made me feel weary and psyched up. I just wanted to get maybe twenty minutes of shut-eye so that I could continue to function. Jeff emerged from the hooch. He relieved me from guard duty. I thought now was the chance to take a quick nap. I acknowledged Jeff. The first thing Jeff said to me was, "Hey, Durham, I got that care package. There are some cookies in there if you want any." I said, "Okay, I just want to get a little sleep." I entered the hooch and noticed a stench in the air. I sniffed and rubbed my nose. The first thing that caught my sight was an airplane-model box with an airplane on it. I looked at what lay beside the box. There was a puffed-up brown bag with a tube of pushed-in airplane glue that was right beside it. The cap was not on it. Jeff came in the hooch behind me.

He said, "Hey, those cookies my mom sent me are pretty good. I said you can try some of them. They are good." Jeff picked up the paper bag and dropped the airplane glue in it. He put the entrance of the bag around his mouth and nose. He inhaled in the bag and then exhaled. I was mesmerized as he went through this act. I was stunned.

Why would a soldier write all the way home and request from his mother to send him a model airplane so that he could sniff the glue that came along with it? What got me was the fact that he would use a care package as a disguise to sniff glue in a combat area. This had caught me by surprise. Here we were engaged in combat, and my so-called squad leader sniffed glue while we were in combat. From that moment on, I lost what respect I had for Jeff because this very act could have put our lives in jeopardy.

I said to him, "You could have put our lives in danger by sniffing that shit." He said, "Rookie, you just got here. So don't judge me." I wanted to pretend that this had never happened. The only thing that Jeff had on me was more time in country.

The days would wear on at this encampment. The time came for Echo Company to move out again. The rumor was we would be going somewhere near the Cambodian border, near the mouth of the Ho Chi Minh trail. We would cut off the supply route going south into the adjacent villages, where Vietcong and NVA soldiers were infiltrating. Sergeant Greely informed us about what was to take place. We converged around Sergeant Greely, once again with First Sergeant Gregory as they stood in the mist of Echo Company. Some of the men were still on guard duty. Sergeant Greely said, "Men, I have an announcement to make. We are going to be moving to a new location! We will be working in and out of a new landing zone named after one of our great generals, Dwight Eisenhower."

We will help them get the firebase in shape, so be ready to do some work. It should be a well-protected LZ. If it's not, we are going to make it that way. So we will be splitting up again into platoons so that we will be able to work in and out of this LZ. I want all of you to realize that we have some work to do and we are also expecting some replacements because we have some guys who are starting to get short. So we're going to need to help these new guys out as much as possible. You know that we never really have a day off while we're out here unless we go on R & R or get put in a body bag."

While in the hooch, I bended on my knees, holding my M.16 upright to pray to God about my situation in respect to the way I would deal with the enemy and any particular soldier. I said, "Protect me, God, yeah, thou I walk in the valley of death, I will fear no evil, thy rod and thy staff they comfort me in the presence of my enemy." I was just glad to leave the area and go somewhere else.

The firebase we were at seemed as if it had the potential of being over run. The fortification of the area was not in good shape as I looked around at open areas where the enemy could get in. A lot of the trees were demolished as they stood charred on their trunks along with the burned-out areas that surrounded them. I wanted to be around an area that had a good fortification along with more fire power.

Eisenhower was one of the better generals of World War II. He became president of the United States. It was the middle of the day when Sergeant Greely and First Sergeant Gregory approached me. I was cleaning my M.16 when the First Sergeant said, "We're going to put you in for another medal, Durham, because of your action at the last firebase. The body counts are starting to increase past the hundreds, and you had a lot to do with that. We need men like you, Durham, so keep doing what you've been doing.

"We also want you and Joe Harris to make some rank. So we got orders to send you all to leadership school. It should be only two or three weeks or maybe not that long and you all will be back with us. This will be another undisclosed location because we don't want Charlie to know what we're doing if you get my drift." I said, "That's all right with me, I just want to do whatever I have to do to get the mission done, even if that means going to leadership school, then that's what I'm going to do." That's the kind of talk I want to hear soldier because we're behind you guys all the way.

"We've got a helo coming in here about 0200 to get you and Joe so that you all can go up to the leadership school and get some more field training so that we can have you men ready to take over a squad when you get back. Plus this is going to put a little more money in your pocket, which I don't think you all will mind, plus combat pay. You can't beat that."

"I can dig that, Sarge."

"The training is going to be intense, so you'll have to watch your selves, and there will also be some written exams you will have to take." Sergeant Greely said, "The army is changing, so we have to change along with it even though we are getting too old for this fucking shit!" I looked at Sergeant Greely and smiled. "We still have a job to do, and that is to get you men ready for combat. So you and Harris get your gear together so you all can get out of here."

The helicopter was on time. It was on the helo pad, waiting for me and Joe to get on board. Sergeant Greely escorted me and Joe to the helicopter. Sergeant Greely told me and Joe that we would be going a little north of where we were at as we boarded the aircraft. The helicopter lifted off; I felt that this was a good ride, just to get away from the new firebase. The ride in this helicopter began to take on another meaning. I wondered if this would help me be a better soldier. My mind would drift back to Leea and the short time that we were together.

This mission started to get more involved because I really never expected to go to any kind of leadership school in Vietnam. Joe and I continued to joke with each other as we took the helicopter ride in stride. Being airmobile meant going to a new destination. It was a challenge.

I still had my death grip on the M.16 as I sat inside the helicopter with a hold on the aircraft while I dangled my feet over top of the skids. What was so good about the trip was the fact that we were not under fire. I knew that we were still easy targets. The machine gunners stayed perched in their seats, ready for anything they felt would be a hindrance for us to get to our destination. They would not speak to each other except through sign language as they looked at the terrain. A motion to each other would let them know what to shoot at.

The helicopter climbed up a ravine as we approached a group of small hilltops, which had open spaces and sparsely scattered trees. It looked like an area that could have been hit by some air strikes.

CHAPTER 10

CULTURE SHOCK

This stretch of mountainside was isolated back in the boonies, which seemed like a ways off from where we had just come from. There appeared to be a little compound, which seemed to be at the side of a small mountain. This still was no landing zone but just a small compound, which had only a few buildings in what appeared to be some sort of infiltration course. The area was protected. There were Vietnamese and American troops guarding the perimeter up in towers along the mountainside. It was obvious to me, but I still wasn't sure how protected it was.

The area was remote. I knew the enemy was always somewhere near. All I knew was that I and Joe had to be prepared. As the helicopter touched down, a squad of about six American soldiers came to greet us. The slender sergeant who appeared was spit-and-polish. The first thing Joe said was, "Okay, Sarge! Where are the gooks? I know they're around here somewhere! That's what I want to know! I know we didn't come all this way for nothing!"

Joe gave the group of soldiers a wide grin with teeth showing as if his statement were a serious joke. The sergeant said, "Don't worry about the gooks around here, they know where to go and where not to go. We have this area covered twenty-four hours a day, and that's the way we are going to keep it. They can try to come in here if they want to, we got something waiting for them that they don't want no part of, which is a whole lot of fire power." Joe smiled and said, "Now that's what I'm talking about! This ain't no picnic, and we want to keep it that way!"

"All right, men, my name is Sergeant Moss, welcome to leadership school! I want you men to follow us so we can show you where you all will be staying. The helicopter started its liftoff. "Watch those helicopter blades. I'd hate to see your heads lying on the ground." The helicopter blades twirled with more speed as the helicopter lifted off the ground.

Joe and I followed the men, who led us to a trail that was headed to the small compound. We made our entrance into the compound that looked like a scale-down version of a boot camp with one building. The sergeant pointed to the building where we would be going and said, "You see that building over there? That's where we're going." We made it to the steps of the building that almost looked like a log cabin. There was a sign on the building that said Training Building.

Sergeant Moss went on to say, "All right, men, listen up. This isn't a difficult school, but you will have to do some work. The kinds of meals that we will have here are c rations. We tried to get the best of the lot." We looked at each other in disgust. There were some mumblings among the soldiers. "As you can see, we have sentries here to keep a watch on things. They will be present throughout your stay here, so let's always be aware of them."

Let's go in to see what the facility is like. It's not home, so you all will just have to make do." We went into the building. As we came through the entrance, it was divided into two sections. We walked farther on into the building. It looked similar to a barracks. On one side of the inside entrance, there was an area that was the sleeping quarters. On the other side of the inside entrance, there was an area that was a classroom.

Sergeant Moss went on to say, "Okay, men, you can go ahead and put up your gear, and I'll be back to let you know what is next." I and Joe found the bunks that we wanted. I chose a bottom bunk, which had wooden planks as a mattress; I would have to use my poncho to get more comfort. I also wanted to be near my gear. I looked at Joe and said, "Well, I guess this will be home for a little while." Joe looked at me from the next bunk over and said, "Yeah, I'm ready to get the hell out of here already! I already see too many gooks around this place."

"Where are they at, Joe?"

"Didn't you see them up in those towers?"

I looked at Joe and said, "I guess we got to deal with it, Joe."

He looked at me and smiled. "What do you mean *we*!" Joe gave me a big grin.

"I know one thing, and that is my M.16 will be on rock and roll."

Joe looked at me and said, "You don't have to tell me that. I'm no fool." Some of the other soldiers in the encampment came into the room. One of the men said, "You guys aren't going to shoot each other up, are you?" I grabbed my M.16 and looked at the trooper while I backed up against him.

I looked at Joe. "Hold me off before I take this guy out." Joe said, "You better hold him off, if you know what I mean." He smiled back at me. Joe asked one of the men, "What kind of a place is this, dude?" The soldier answered, "Oh, this is just another shit hole." Joe then replied, "Oh, you can say that again!" The soldier replied, "I'll be getting out of here tomorrow, so I don't give a fuck! I guess it's all right for a little while, but I'm ready to get the fuck out of here as the soldier walked out the room." Joe then replied, "I heard that! You take it easy."

Sergeant Moss came back in the room again and said, "All right, men, I want you to follow me over here so that I can give you a little orientation." Me and Joe followed the sergeant into the empty class room along with a few other men. Some were already waiting in the classroom. I found a desk seat second from the front; I wanted to hear clearly what the sergeant had to say. Joe went to sit in the back of the class. I could see Joe was not happy being there as he sat down in his disgruntled mood with his arms folded. The sergeant went straight to the front, where he sat on a wooden table that seemed as if it was made for him. He then said, "First of all, I'd like to welcome the new men who just came in for the leadership school.

"We have a pretty efficient program here. This is not one of those shake-and-bake schools like they have back in the states. Here you get to train around actual combat conditions. This school has only been here a little while, so we have been able to put out some hard fives and send them back to their units. If you don't know what a hard five is, it's a sergeant that has made it in combat. This process is what you make it. We will not be holding any hands.

"A lot of you men have already been in combat situations. So to some of you, this won't be that new. To some of you, this will be new because you were stuck back in the rear. So pay attention and you should get through this all right. We have some goals here, and I want you to keep them in mind. The main goal is to earn your stripes. When you leave here, you will get those stripes, and there will be nothing hard about it if you use your head.

"Our main objectives will be to get you through the make shift obstacle course that you will be going on while you're here at this camp. We'll also be doing some classroom work to complement with your work out side. I want you to understand what I'm saying. Do you hear me?" The response from a few of the troops was, "Yes, sir!"

"So if you have any questions, don't be afraid to ask me because I'm not going anywhere. I'll be right here, so let's do what we have to do so we can get out of here and get back to our units. This is possible. I know you men can do it.

"Another thing that I want to mention is the fact that this is a two-week program. That seems like a short time, but it could seem longer if we have to engage our enemy. So we have to depend on our men in the towers to let us know what's going on in our surrounding area. They will be our main source of security right now unless they need some more help. We will be training with live ammo, this is not a partial boot camp like back at home. This is Vietnam!

"The order of the day is being up by three in the morning ready to go to start off the day. We will have some inside instruction to talk about our enemy and explain what kind of enemy we are dealing with. So you'll have to put on your thinking caps and decipher this information as fast as you can. We will go over some things that you might have questions about or don't understand. We will take a series of about three exams to get the knowledge of what we will be learning here. Your aptitude and attitude will be very important. You will have to have a passing score to get your sergeant stripes. The idea of this class is to send you out as squad leaders, and that is what we intend to do. I'm not going to lie to you, some of you will not make it. That is just the way it is."

Sergeant Moss yelled out, "Specialist Peters! Wake up!" The soldier jumped up in his desk startled. "There will be no sleeping while you are in my classroom. Do you understand that, son?" The soldier answered, "Yes, sir!" I looked over at Joe as he laughed about what had just happened. Sergeant Moss repeated, "We are here for one reason, and that is to become better soldiers. If you were out in the field and were caught sleeping, your throat would get cut. In this classroom, you can be faced with an Article 15 and a stripe taken away. All right, gentlemen in the back, have a seat."

There was some paperwork that was passed out to get some basic information from us. It was some information about family and so on. Sergeant Moss handed out pencils. He said, "As soon as you finish that, you can go and get some chow because we will be going outside to get some more instructions. So don't get comfortable and take a nap because we have some work to do." At this point, I didn't quite know how to accept what I and Joe had gotten into. All I knew was that I had to do my best and learn as much about combat to achieve my goal of becoming a sergeant. Sergeant Moss wasn't just any kind of sergeant but a sergeant who could be respected because you wouldn't get these kinds of stripes back in the states. By getting stripes in Vietnam meant you really earned them because you were in a combat theater. This was where the real fighting was. The stripes meant a lot to me. All Joe talked about was getting out of the camp so we could do what we had to do to go home. I continued to tease Joe about his big head and other characteristics about him.

We would play it off. I would use Joe to get cigarettes from because he had brought a little supply of kools with him that he had gotten from somewhere before we got to the training camp. The c rations were really the same, but there seemed to be some extra fruit that was discovered in the cans, along with some chocolate bars. The beans and franks still came in handy also. The eating breaks would take no more than about ten minutes.

We were constant in checking our weapons, which gave me and Joe assurance. At times we get a catnap, but not for long. I just wanted to get this ordeal over so that I could get back to the unit. By not making any waves at this point would confirm that I was on track. What Joe had on his mind didn't affect the way I wanted to approach this mission. I was still fond of Joe.

He could always get a laugh out of me even though we were subjected to the circumstances of being at the training facility and in Vietnam. Joe was like a big teddy bear, but you had to know how far to go with him. He was uncomfortable in the classroom. He would rather be in some action and get it over with. It made no sense to Joe; he just happened to be picked to come to leadership school. Joe and I would often be right by each other as we went through the different stations of leadership school.

The school had a specific routine that we would go through. The first few days were spent inside and outside the classroom, along with the lunch break, while we smoked cigarettes. We would go out in thick brush to see if we recognized the different tactics that the Vietcong would use. There was one instance when Joe spotted a wire on a fake trail that was used as a booby trap. Sergeant Moss congratulated Joe on what he discovered. The day normally started with instruction on the kind of soldier the Vietnamese was and what his habitat was like as far as living in his country. It was how the Americans looked upon them as an adversary.

We were told in the classroom about how to distinguish an NVA from a Vietcong. Sergeant Moss would tell the class that their dress was different in comparison to one another. They would distinguish themselves as peasants by day and get into their Vietcong disguise when it turned dark. Many times, the civilian Vietnamese would observe the American soldier by day to get the necessary information to give to the enemy. They would talk about troop strength and where the American troops would move next.

We were shown different items that the enemy would have in their possession. The Vietcong in many instances would have on rubber sandals that they would wear and some other type of clothing that looked like loincloth or pieces of an NVA uniform that they had confiscated. The AK-47 was part of his apparel, along with an RPG or some type of explosive device that he made up. He would also carry his food items, which consisted of rice and seeds along with grain and opium. He was equipped to move swiftly. The opium was used to keep them awake and help with pain from a wound. Sergeant Moss would talk about the Vietnamese soldier's ability to travel in small groups that were used for harassment to lure American troops into an ambush.

Sergeant Moss also talked about how the regiments of NVA regulars would communicate with the Vietcong by using flanking moves to confront the American troops that were large American line companies. There were maps of different regions of Vietnam. Every day at the training camp, we would be given information about different things that pertained to the terrain of Vietnam along with the different types of landscapes that would appear in those regions.

There were a number of drawings of rice paddies and rubber plantations that existed in the country. There also was a map drawn of Cambodia, where supplies would come down through tributaries off the Ho Chi Minh trail. While in the classroom, I would glance over at Joe. Sometimes Joe would appear to be in a nod but would snap out of it once he realized that he was about to go to sleep.

Following the classroom time, Sergeant Moss would tell everybody to grab his M.16 because we would be spending the rest of the day on the infiltration course. The infiltration course would be about two or three miles in diameter with different kinds of scenery that was in Vietnam. Sergeant Moss wanted to let you know what it was like to be in different combat situations. Sergeant Moss would give different scenarios to us with different views of what could possibly happen that was unexpected. He would talk about how a soldier would react to certain situations that presented themselves. The ability to detect what the enemy was trying to do was the objective. There would be a situation where an enemy soldier would pretend to be gravely wounded to lure you into an ambush.

Sergeant Moss took a small unit of us down a trail, which appeared to be about a mile long. It was in a valley of elephant grass. There would be a silhouette of an enemy soldier ahead. Sergeant Moss addressed this situation. He said, "Now what would you do in a situation like this? First of all, you would want to see if this soldier was by himself after you kill him because he would probably be attached to a unit that is not far away. If you were a mortarman, you would probably have to prep the area where his comrades could possibly be. You would fire in a circumference of 180 degrees with your mortars."

This scenario entered my mind as if I were right there in the action. Everybody was in a staggered formation, with M.16s pointed in opposite directions. Sergeant Moss made everybody form a circle around him. He took a piece of bamboo and made a half circle in the ground. Sergeant Moss said, "You see this half circle? That is the enemy." He moved the bamboo stick up to the middle of the circle. You don't want to get caught in what is called a 360 or horseshoe that could be closed in around you." He then completed the circle.

"You don't want the enemy to get the advantage. Now let me tell you about the dead soldier. You move forward and find out what the dead soldier has on him that would be of importance. Never put yourself out on a limb. That's where the enemy has an advantage." Sergeant Moss said this with conviction in his voice that was not hard for me not to believe. These kinds of lessons would go on for the next two weeks.

Sergeant Moss would tell us about certain gestures of the enemy and the type of tactics they would use. The ability to out think the enemy was clear because the survival of your squad would depend on it. There also was additional information on how they would use pungy stakes and other unconventional measures that would harm their opponent. The fact that they could be well camouflaged on different hillsides and along small ravines was also taught.

We looked at spider holes where the tunnel rats would go. Volunteers were used for that dangerous task. I wanted no part in dealing with the underground war. There were also hidden wires that would be used to detonate live grenades, which had to be detected. We would take roads that we thought the enemy hadn't traveled. You would have to put your machete to use. There were also classes on map readings and what to do in case you got captured. The troops were told by Sergeant Moss the first thing you needed to do to keep from getting captured is not to get captured at all. That seemed to be the best advice for me because I felt someone was going to die in order for me to get captured, and that meant a whole lot of the enemy.

The final day had come, and it was time for Joe and me to get back to our unit. I was anxious to find out what was going on with my unit and find out how everybody was doing. Washing parts of your body in a creek was starting to get kind of old. I didn't want to expose myself just to get some dirt off to wash my fatigues with soap, so I would wash while my fatigues were still on. All I wanted to do now was get back to my unit and do the rest of my tour.

We took our final test before we were told if we passed. I could see Joe sweating as we finished the last exam. I felt a lot of the questions were based on what we had learned at the encampment. The test was not complicated. My test was completed. At this point most of the soldiers that took the test were finished. As soon as the last man finished, Sergeant Moss made an announcement. "I'd like to let you know it's been a pleasure serving with you men, so let's go out there and get Charlie! A fail and pass list will be posted to the rear of the barracks."

At that moment, Joe and I knew that we had to get our gear together so that we could meet the helicopters. The final thing that we did was check to see if we had passed the test. We approached the wall where the test results were posted. There was a little bit of trepidation when we approached the wall while I adjusted my rucksack over my shoulder with weapon in hand. The list wasn't that long. It revealed that I made sergeant. Joe's name appeared under the failure column. I looked at Joe and said, "Come on, man, let's go! We got to get out of here!" Sergeant Moss told me that I should get my stripes in a few weeks. The ride on the helicopter was one of some regret because Joe didn't make sergeant, but I knew he had a role to fill now that required him to act like a leader. The flight was silent most of the way to LZ Ike.

Joe shook off what had just happened. He knew he was still the same soldier, and nothing was going to change that. All he wanted to do was get back to Louisiana in one piece. The big LZ below looked like everybody was getting it ready for battle. It appeared that the perimeter was intact. The gun posts appeared to be set up in their proper places. The artillery pieces were positioned at all angles in reference to where the enemy might be coming from.

There was a sign posted that said LZ Ike. Empty ammo boxes and pallets were scattered around the helicopter pad. Everything seemed in a little disarray but in order. I visualized being on patrol as I looked out at the terrain on the helicopter. Sweat poured down my face. The ambush I envisioned was the same one Sergeant Moss talked about, which was the one where we were encircled by the enemy. I soon came back to my conscious. I still was not keen on going back out on patrol but would do it if necessary.

As soon as Joe and I got off the helicopter, we located a soldier who was from Echo Company. I asked the soldier where Echo Company had set up. The soldier pointed over to the northern part of the perimeter, where there were three bunkers located on the berm. There were also partially completed mortar pits that were located near the bunkers. The mortars were the main instruments that stood out.

The stakes were set up and ready to be fired on enemy targets. There was a limited amount of mortar rounds out of their boxes in the mortar pits. The bunkers were positioned about fifty yards out in between the mortar pits along with .50- and .60-caliber machine guns sitting on top of them. I wanted to find out where Sergeant Greely was. I asked a soldier where he might be. The soldier replied, "Oh, I see you guys made it back okay." Then he said, "Sergeant Greely is out in the field on patrol, they should be back in a few hours." The sergeant stripes I got would be on a washed fatigue shirt that I found in a pile of clean fatigues in the mortar pit. I looked at the sergeant stripes in amazement.

It wasn't long before Sergeant Greely made his appearance. He looked his usual self. He was gung ho as ever. He had a patrol of about eight men with him. I didn't see Smitty or Harry. It appeared that they did not go out on that patrol. Sergeant Greely looked at me and said, "I'm glad you guys made it back." He asked, "How'd everything go?" I told him that I made sergeant. A smile came over Sergeant Greely's face. He said, "I knew you could do it, son. Top will be glad to hear about it." He then asked about Joe. "Hey! Joe! How did you do?" Joe replied as he heard the conversation while he stood nearby. "I didn't make it, Sarge." Sergeant Greely looked Joe up and down and said, "You're a big fella! You can take it. There will be other schools you can go to.

"We still got a job for you to do, so don't worry, big guy." Joe gave him that usual smile. Sergeant Greely went on to say, "We haven't been here that long, but I can still smell Charlie. From the communication that we've been getting, they're going to try and over run us. It's already happened to a few units up north, so welcome to LZ Ike. We got a lot of work to do! This LZ is in piss-poor shape! But we are going to get it together. We will get some hot meals in here for you guys.

"I'm also expecting some new recruits to replace some of our people. We need a new LT, but we haven't got one yet. Captain Wright is looking into the matter, so we still have work to do. We just have to use what we have. So far right now, we're going to need a squad leader to take over a mortar squad, and it looks like that's going to be you, Durham. We'll have to get a few guys to help you out so that we can get this unit in order." The new men began to appear. They were two rugged midwesterners. One was named Scott, and the other one's name was Jason. We began to work together to form our squad. They seemed to be indifferent as we went about our necessary chores.

The monsoon was still prevalent. The pallets were made into a bed to help keep us out of the water as we slept. The plastic from some of the boxed .81-millimeter rounds was used to cover them up along with ourselves. Rats swam around as they tried to get to higher ground. I was frightened by the ones that would crawl on top of me while I tried to get some sleep. Aluminum roofs were drapped over two by fours to give us a roof. Plastic was put between sand bags to keep the rain out of the hooch. The recent monsoon appeared to have subsided, but the end seemed to be nowhere in sight. It hindered getting the LZ in the physical shape that it needed to be in, but there had to be taken extra measures to assure that it would be ready for combat because the adversary was going through the same thing. My squad started to take shape. In the hooches, the water was so bad from the monsoon that it had to be bailed out with canteens.

When you are new in a country, your attention span is in awe because you are in conditions that have not been imposed upon you. The guard duty was still four on and four off. It was important for you to keep your eyes open. When night came, you really wanted to see what was going on. Soldiers started to take c4 out of the claymore mines to heat up food. It could have posed a threat but was being ignored because the men wanted something warm to eat. I would deal with the cold c rations until the mess tent was ready for hot food.

I told the new men not to expose fire at night because it would give away your position, even though guys would use flashlights while out on night patrol, which I thought was crazy. The monsoon season was soon over. The sun raised the heat as soldiers discarded their top fatigue shirt. They even started to get tans, which were even possible for some of the black troops. To know your company area of the LZ was almost like a community thing as you got to know some of the guys for a short while in your unit. I really didn't want to get too close to the guys who got short. It just seemed to me that these guys gained respect because of the short amount of time that they had left in the country. There became times when you didn't want to hear about anybody that got short because they were supposed to leave sooner than you. The cooks had on their white uniforms while they worked in the mess tent and went about their work to get food prepared.

There were also rations of beer and soda that started to come into the perimeter on a weekly basis. These refreshments would always be hot, and neither of them seemed to taste any better than the other. I would prefer the sodas. The sodas seemed to give you energy. Some guys preferred the beer. You would get a beer or two sodas. They would try to distribute the beverages out in a fair manner. These beverages were usually traded off for one another. I traded off my beer also because it dehydrated me.

CHAPTER 11

ESCAPE ON R & R

There was a soldier in my mortar squad who would barter sodas and beer. His name was Bill. Bill was older than the rest of the troops in the unit. He was also an old white trash from the Midwest. He had dark hair, freckles on his face, and olive spotted skin, which appeared when he took off his shirt. He walked with a partially hunched back as he walked around in the mortar pit one afternoon. He was now part of my mortar squad. He approached me while I wiped down the mortar and said, "Hey, you got some beer? I've got a few cans of beer and some sodas. Do you want to trade some sodas for beer? Hey, I heard you just made sergeant."

"Yeah, I'm the one, what about it. Didn't you ask me something about some beer?"

"Yeah, I want some beer if you got it. Who the hell do you think I'm asking?" I stood up in front of him and laughed. I soon hunched down to go inside the hooch to get the beer. I soon came back out of the hooch with the beer. "Here, man, take the beer and give me your sodas." Bill responded, "When you get some more beer, let me know."

"Okay, I'll do that." Bill smiled with his dingy-looking teeth and said, "You got some sodas coming." Bill took the cans of beer and laid them in the mortar pit. I was starting to get to know some of the other soldiers in my unit. I found out that I was the youngest sergeant in the unit at nineteen. I knew that some of the soldiers in my unit were in their midtwenties and thirties. I would often be challenged. It was especially by Bill and another soldier that was called Red, who was in the mortar squad next to mine.

Red was from the Midwest also, by the way of Indiana. He was a little taller than I was and a little heavier. His hair was bright red. There always seemed to be an atmosphere of machismo to Red. The posturing would start from a playful shove and then turn into a wrestling match. I would not back down to the challenges. We as young soldiers would posture, and then the contest would begin. It was a matter of who would dominate the most. It turned out most of the time to be me. I was the champion and wanted to keep it that way. My physical strength was a factor in me winning all the wrestling matches.

This would go on days at a time, with me always having the upper hand, slamming my opponents to the ground. It was a matter of getting the right grip so that I would be able to slam the weaker soldier down to the ground. One day, Red caught on and turned the tables on me. He finally won a match. Bill never did win a match even though he would try you while having too many beers. I shook Red's hand for the one win that he got. The wrestling matches would never happen again.

It was good to know the kinds of guys you would be fighting with because you never knew when we would need one another despite the fact that there was a little horseplay but friendly.

The medic made his presence known in Echo Company while at LZ Ike. He introduced himself to me as Specialist Jesse. Jesse came into LZ Ike with a different attitude than any of the other soldiers that I met. Maybe it had something to do with the fact that he was a medic. He was kind of a medium build but slender, with medium brown hair. He had a slight and slender build. He was quiet and reserved as he carried his medical pack strapped over his shoulder. He had his flight vest attached to his body along with his steel pot on his head. He mingled with the troops to see how they were doing.

What was peculiar about him was the fact that he was a contentious objector. While I ate some c rations one day, the medic was walking around the perimeter, getting acquainted with some of the soldiers. He just so happened to walk by my mortar pit. I was wearing my steel pot and flight vest. I asked the medic about his M.16, which was colored with yellow flowers all up and down the stock and barrel. I said, "Hey, Doc! Why do you have your M.16 covered with all those flowers on it?"

Doc said, "I'm a flower child, and I believe in peace, I'm here to help the wounded."

"I notice you don't have a clip in your rifle."

"You're right. I don't need a clip because I don't believe in killing."

At that point I said, "You are a brave man. I couldn't do what you're doing, that's just the way I feel." The medic looked at me and smiled. "If there's anything I can do for you, let me know." The medic's hooch was located about twenty feet from the mortar pit. He walked over to his hooch as if he went to get something.

From time to time, the line companies would come from out of the field to get some rest and spend a little time at Landing Zone Ike. One afternoon while I and my squad were going over some things about the mortar, I saw a line company emerge from the boonies, with about 120 soldiers. They snaked up inside the perimeter, making their presence known. They always were a dirty bunch of guys, unshaven and dirty. They came through the artillery pieces, headed for some of the bunkers for guard duty.

They were weary from the ordeal of being in the boonies for weeks at a time. Their dirty look of weariness was expressed through their faces and the slowness of their walk as they moved within the perimeter. They looked for some of the portable showers that were available inside the perimeter. One of the first soldiers that I noticed was Smitty. We had not seen Smitty in weeks. I noticed that he didn't have his M.16.

He was being escorted in handcuffs by two MPs who were carrying sidearms. They also had their M.16s, walking by his side. I approached Smitty and said, "What's going on, Smitty?" Smitty looked at me with a sneer on his face. It seemed as if he were stoned on something. A haze was in his eyes, which seemed like he was in a trance. He didn't look good.

I thought for a minute maybe Smitty had gotten hold of some opium. I felt that Smitty wasn't himself other than being sarcastic. Staying in the field had finally gotten to him. He seemed angry as he stood with his wrinkled and dusty fatigues, which had jungle all over them. He said, "I'm getting the fuck out of the field. I refuse to walk point anymore!"

"What's this all about, Smitty?"

"It's about me and Sergeant Greely. He transferred me because I didn't want to walk point anymore. I told him I was getting too short to walk point. I told him to take me off it! So I'm getting ready to go to Long Binh Jail. I'm ready to do some time. I'm tired of being out here in this fucking field!" Harry was not too far behind as he walked up to me. He also looked disheveled.

Harry stumbled toward me as Smitty headed out to the helicopter pad. His face was swollen, and his eyes almost bulged out of his head. He told me in a whisper, "I'm getting out of the field too. They're going to send me back to the rear so I can get some help. They think something is wrong with me, but all I did was eat a bar of soap. You see what it did to me. They're going to have to find out what's going on with me." And then there was a little gleam in his eyes.

"I might be going back to the world. I don't belong out here, Durham. I'm ready to go home. I don't care how short I am. I want to get out of this fucking place. I'm not going to jail like that dumb-ass Smitty. They're going to send me home." Harry caught up with his platoon. I never did see him or Smitty again. Harry held up the black power fist with his black shoe bracelet going up toward the sky and said, "Peace, brother! I'll see you back in the world!"

While back at the platoon of Echo Company, Joe managed to get the job of being on the .50-caliber machine gun. He would be positioned at a bunker that was right in front of my mortar pit. He felt this position was better than going out into the field on patrols. I would talk to him from time to time and joke around when we got the opportunity. It was hot most of June at LZ Ike, but on the eve of the nineteenth, the air was full of anticipation of something possibly happening. Guard duty seemed to have been working in sequence. I liked to have guard duty right before midnight. I could only guess at what time it was. I would develop a sense of the time because of the shape of the moon and its brightness.

I was anxious to get my turn over with after midnight. After being relieved, I was still uneasy as I tossed and turned over on my makeshift bed on top of pallets. On this night, at about three in the morning, I was shaken with the thud of incoming rounds and was awoken by those dreaded words. "Incoming!" *Boom . . . Boom, zzzzzzzzzzzzzzzzz, boom, thump! Thump!* In succession—*boom boom kak kak kak*—the sound of the AK-47 rounds made their appearance with green and red tracers being seen going over different positions all around the perimeter. There was a mixture of recoilless rifles along with the sound of grenades and mortars being popped.

Contact was being made with the main enemy fire coming from about two miles out. Joe opened up on the .50 caliber along with additional .60 machine gun fire along the front middle right and left flanks of the perimeter. The sky was lit up. Everything was coming in as a barrage of rounds, which impacted inside the perimeter.

I grabbed his M.16 just in case I would have to fight close in. Everyone in the LZ was up as they scuffled around. Some soldiers were in a low crawl as they made their way to cover. We also crawled in the mortar pit to get in our positions. The mortar was already calibrated and ready to go. All it needed were the .81 rounds. I glanced up quickly at the trip flares, which illuminated the sky from the north, along with the sounds of the whistling rockets that were making their way into the perimeter.

I told Scott and Jason to stay down low and start getting rounds ready while I went over to where the rounds lay. I looked up quickly again to see where the mortar stakes were in comparison to where the attack was coming from. I could see flashes about two miles or less out toward the north.

I soon started the process of sending rounds out with the right amount of charges taken off to give me the distance I needed. The men in the squad followed my lead. It was only a matter of seconds. The response was immediate once again as I dropped five rounds on enemy positions. I yelled once again, "Come on, hurry up!" I took the rounds from the feeder and dropped them down the tube in steady sequence in a matter of seconds. I didn't care how hot the tube had gotten as long as it was in the proper position.

The base plate shook as the rounds met the firing pin. The rounds blasted out of the tube with no restraint. The objective was to put out as many rounds as possible, and that is exactly what my squad did.

The enemy could barely be seen as the flashes from the outgoing mortar rounds were met with counter fire. Sergeant Greely appeared from out of headquarters along with another soldier staying low while coming toward the mortar pit. He said, "Durham, you see where it's coming from!"

"Yeah, Sarge!"

"The targets are about two miles or less out. Keep up that fire power, son, don't let up. I'm going to need one of your men to go to a bunker with your 16 in case they want to come closer! I also have a new man that's going to help you out, Durham." I turned and glanced at Sergeant Greely.

I noticed the soldier that was with him. "I'm going to let this new man stay here to help you, Sergeant Durham! His name is PFC Riker. I have to go, Durham, so I'm leaving him with you. So let him know what to do!" In all the commotion, my most concern was getting as much fire power out as possible. I looked at the new soldier and said, "Hey, man, you got to get down and help with the ammo!" I pointed to Scott. "You see what he's doing, we need to open those ammo boxes to get more rounds out!" You could tell the recruit was new because of his crisp, clean-looking fatigues.

The trip flares continued to illuminate. The new recruit had dark hair and a new flight vest and steel pot on. I yelled at him once again. "Did you hear me, I said get down. We're being hit!" Then I noticed the fear on the soldier's face. He had become petrified. The trooper held his M.16 to his chest. His face turned an ash-looking white. This new recruit went into a thousand-mile stare. He didn't react to the situation at hand. I knew then that this man was no good to me because he wasn't going to fight. I yelled over to Sergeant Greely and said, "Hey! Sergeant Greely, we got a problem!" Sergeant Greely turned around and headed back to the mortar pit in the midst of incoming rounds. Sergeant Greely said, "What do you mean you have a problem?"

"Something is wrong with the new man. He's not following my orders. He won't fight."

Sergeant Greely replied, "What do you mean he won't fight?" Then the sergeant turned to the man and said, "Son, what is wrong with you?" The soldier just stood there without saying a word, with the same look in his eyes that never went away. He laid down his M.16. At this point Sergeant Greely and I didn't know if this man could talk. Sergeant Greely responded to him, with incoming still making its presence all around us. "Son, we're going to have to get you out of here! Get your weapon, you're coming with me to headquarters. You don't need to be out here, so let's go!" Sergeant Greely grabbed the soldier by the arm and led him out of the mortar pit toward the big bunker to the rear of the mortar pit.

Being out of the line of fire was the best thing for the soldier because all he would be was an exposed target. At this point, I still had to get as many rounds as I could to the threatening positions that seemed like they weren't letting up. Once again it was a two-man show in the mortar pit, and the fire power still had to be in the continuous mode regardless of what had just happened. The mortar tube's glow of being used with effectiveness showed. I made sure that there was no let up as long as I was at the helm. I continued to walk the mortar rounds within the two- to three-mile radius. The rounds continued to fall in the midst of the enemy. I felt that you had to let the enemy know that I meant business, and that meant giving him more than his medicine.

The enemy was not going to escape the wrath of the mortar. I started walking rounds across the enemy land scape as I turned the adjustments on the mortar so that I could move the rounds horizontally as well as vertically, making a cross configuration that was perfect, while the enemy didn't know which way to go. The .81-millimeter rounds were affecting 100 to 250 enemy soldiers. There was no reason to let up as long as I, Jason, and Scott had the rounds to accommodate them.

It seemed like eternity when these battles would take place. It was when the enemy considered his efforts fruitless that he would wait to fight another day. It was under the cover of darkness that the Vietnamese soldier felt he could operate. The enemy still felt he could do some severe damage to LZ Ike. But once daylight came, the enemy knew that this was the best time to hide because of the additional fire power from the air, which in a lot of instances could also happen at night with the gunships.

It was hard for the enemy to deal with. The next process was to get ready for it to happen all over again, so there was no hesitation of using this time to get the mortar pit ready again for more engagement. The smoldering atmosphere would be gotten through as the fog of the previous fight lifted. Assessments were taken to see how much damage was done. Bodies were being dragged away, and some shallow graves were made as the enemy retreated.

Jesse, the medic, tended to the wounded, which were not in my squad. The constant praying, along with the constant fighting, was paying off for me. I wanted to keep it that way. I wanted to find the Catholic priest that I had seen at certain times around the perimeter. Sooner or later I would catch up with the priest. There was need for special prayer because the battles started to increase with intensity. I felt that this landing zone should have another name other than LZ Ike because it definitely was a target that the enemy wanted. I felt my mortar squad was determined not to let that happen. My leadership skills would be displayed, especially after I made sergeant. The dust was still clearing as the morning became more apparent.

The LZ had emerged from a period of disarray, which made it look even more out of order, except most of the guns were still in place. There were some bunkers and hooches that were missed by the enemy. I saw Joe cleaning his .50-caliber machine gun from the bunker he was stationed at. He checked the gun parts to see if they were still in place. The mortar was still in good shape. I yelled over to Joe, "You all right over there, soldier?"

Joe replied in his usual way, "You damn right! I'm all right! Sarge told me to hold and keep a good look out and don't fire until I saw the whites in their eyes because mine are wide open." I looked at him and laughed. "Boy, you still crazy." But in reality it wasn't a laughing matter because we didn't know how long the enemy would persist. The fire power we used to align with the heavy artillery was an important matter. The coordinates were ample enough to be used at the kind of range where the enemy was.

This direction of fire had to be done without impunity regardless of the crafty Vietnamese soldier and his tactics. I soon saw Sergeant Greely. I asked him, "What happened to that soldier that froze?"

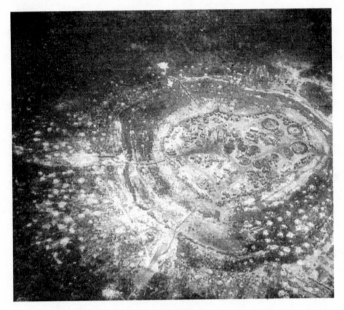

L Z Ike

"Oh, he's just one of those New York City boys who have no business out here. So we're going to see about sending him back to the rear on the next chopper out of here."

"Yeah, you're right, Sarge, this is no place for somebody like him." While the conversation took place, a chopper arrived. The mortified soldier who Sergeant Greely and I were talking about was being escorted out to the chopper that just arrived. Soon the chopper was off again in the horizon with the cowardly soldier.

Patrols headed outside the perimeter to do their search-and-destroy missions. There was more talk about doing night patrols. The daylight patrols were bad enough, but to add night patrols was dangerous. And it also had consequences on morale because by not using any kind of night vision equipment, it made it hard to see where the enemy was.

The snipers were being introduced to the latest night vision scopes on their weapons, but this wasn't doing any good for the soldiers that had to go out at night on foot patrol. The only thing you had to go by at night would be to use the moon as much as possible with the use of flares and the stars that would be of some help, depending on what kind of night it was. I thought the night patrols were insane. Sergeant Greely told me that the replacement they were looking for was coming to the unit any day now to make my squad more efficient. I didn't mind the extra man power because it was always an asset, especially if the man was focused on fighting. It wasn't long before the new replacement would arrive.

Ishmal came into the squad one afternoon off the dusty chopper pad, which started to look beaten up because of its use. I saw the recruit come off the chopper with his fatigue shirt open in what appeared like a relatively new pair of fatigues. The fatigues had a moderate amount of dirt on them. The dirt was just enough to know that the soldier still had the new appearance of just coming from the states. He appeared as a new soldier who had just arrived in the country.

His unworn boots were a testament that they had not been tested on the grounds of Vietnam. His complexion was a bronze tinge. He didn't get this look from being in the states or in Vietnam. It seemed to me that he had gotten this look from another part of the world. Perhaps it was from an Arab country. Sergeant Greely greeted the new soldier as he made his way through the swirling debris from the chopper that was starting to make its exit.

As they walked into the landing zone, Sergeant Greely carried on a conversation with the new recruit. Sergeant Greely pointed toward my mortar pit. It was obvious that this new soldier would join my mortar squad. It was obvious because Sergeant Greely had been talking about getting me a replacement. As they got closer, I could see that the new soldier's features were Arabic, which stood out more clearly. His demeanor seemed to be sassy and confident.

He was well built and looked like he had just gotten out of advanced infantry training. He appeared as a man who looked like he had been lifting weights in his off time. I really didn't know how strong he was physically.

I stood near the mortar when Sergeant Greely introduced me to him. "Durham, this is your new man. His name is Ishmal, and I have assigned him to your squad. So you do what is necessary to get this man adjusted because this is a combat zone that we need every man in it to do his job." I looked him up and down. "How you doing, recruit?" I got into the habit of trying to check out a soldier as closely as possible because of my recent encounter with new soldiers.

"How is everything going, Durham?" I looked at Sergeant Greely and said, "So far it's been quiet, Sarge, but I don't expect it to stay this way for too long." Then I asked Ishmal, "How long you been in country?" Ishmal responded in his slight Arabic and English accent, "I've been here a few weeks now. I came here from California."

"What part of California?"

He said, "I live near Los Angeles down near the beach. I have some relatives out there."

"You look like you have some of that California tan."

He answered, "I am also from Israel. Yeah, I spent a lot of time out on the beach with some beautiful American women. The American woman seems to like Arab men because we look like good lovers." On that note, Sergeant Greely said, "Okay, Durham, I need to go and check with Top, so I'll see you all later. Also, I'd like to let you know, Durham, that we put you in for another medal." I responded, "I just want to make it home, Sarge." Sergeant Greely replied, "What we need are men that can fight so that we all can go home in one piece."

Me and the soldiers getting awards

"We'll do what we got to do, Sarge." Ishmal went over to a corner of the mortar pit. He took his equipment off his back. He sat down near the hooch. He laid his M.16 to the side. He then pulled out a cigarette. He got the cigarette from a pack of Camels that he had in his pocket. Ishmal took off his steel pot. His hair was jet-black, along with the dark features that went along with his skin.

He pulled the bandoliers from off his shoulders. He opened his shirt and proceeded to light his Camel cigarette. The next thing he said was, "Where do you get some food around here? I'm hungry!" I pointed over to the mess tent that was about two hundred yards on the left side of the mortar pit. I said, "They'll be serving chow over there pretty soon. I don't know if we'll get any hot meals coming in here or not today, we just have to wait and see. The food's nothing to write home about, but it is good to have something hot to eat. Sometimes, those cooks look out for you."

The ongoing relationship with Ishmal was a work in progress because it seemed like the conversation would always center on him. Ishmal's behavior became questionable. It had something to do with his demeanor and his disappearing acts. I felt he was up to something but didn't quite know what it was. I had become very suspicious of the soldier from Israel who happened to be of Arab descent. I would be at the mortar pit 24-7. He really didn't have any reason to venture out inside the perimeter at this period of his tour. I wanted to get to know my men in the squad to build a camaraderie that I felt was needed to keep all of them alive. This would not always be the case if you were in battle with your men. All I wanted my men to do was just to concentrate on being a warrior. You still had to be aware of the soldier that could put your life in danger because of the fear that could play tricks on you. So whenever there was a lull in the fighting, you would try to get to know the soldier that fought next to you despite the hardship. When a soldier has more time than you, it's hard to talk to him because you know that he has a short way to go, and you do not want to do anything to hinder him from getting home because you had less time than he did. It was a form of respect and admiration you would develop for the soldier.

It was also hard to get to know a soldier who had just got in the country because he still had to be tutored and weaned into the battlefield. Also, being able to get rest would mean a lot to you because you had to have energy for the next battle. It was the ideas of not letting fatigue set in and interfere with your fighting ability. I preferred to get things done in preparation for the next battle.

Ishmal had become friends with Scott and Jason, who all were subordinate to me and had some time to do. The clique had been formed between them, and it seemed like I wasn't privy to a lot of the conversations that would take place between these soldiers. My stripes started to show more division than I anticipated between me and the men who were in my squad. Maybe it was my youth that was cause for descent.

CHAPTER 12

LZ IKE

It seemed to be alienation until it was time to fight, which was okay with me. I knew it was important for us to act as a team and a squad. The situation of battle had to always be adhered to. To prepare for battle was a part of an effort that was put in by all of the squad. I continued to notice the soldier's subtle behavior. To give instructions was put on deaf ears, or was it my imagination?

One day, I was talking to Ishmal after he had gotten some mail. Arrogance was present as I sat breaking open ammo boxes with mortars in them. We both faced each other as he sat on another ammo box next to the hooch. Ishmal started the conversation. "Do you know that I came to America from Israel to live in California? My family wanted to move there because it was a better place to live for my family. I could have joined the army in Israel and fought for my people who were being mistreated by the Israeli army."

I then asked him, "So why didn't your family stay in Israel?" Ishmal replied, "They wanted to protect me. Everybody told my father that America was a place he could bring his family so that we could be safe. I was young. I should have moved back to help my people." He then went on to say, "I was young, and there was nothing I could do about it. My fight isn't here but in Israel. So here I am in the U.S. Army fighting this fucked-up war when I could be in my own country. You're an RA, you wanted to join the army. I made a mistake, and now I can't get out of it."

Ishmal pulled out some pictures from his fatigue pockets that he had just received from mail call. "I want you to take a look at these pictures. I have always liked American girls, especially the girls out in California. I just love blond girls, they do anything I say. See these girls, they all think I should be a movie star. I told them maybe I will be one someday. They just love me so much." He then showed me his muscles as he stood up with his shirt off.

I didn't know why he tried to impress me. I also had abs and other muscles that were just as pronounced as his. He reiterated as he showed me the pictures once again while laughing. He said, "They want me so bad. They have never seen someone so handsome as me." As soon as the conversation was over, Ishmal would disappear and not be seen for several hours. Ishmal smoked pot as a pastime when he was absent from my presence. He sat in one of the bunkers on the perimeter, where he inhaled the smoke with a smile on his face as other soldiers looked on.

Sergeant Greely approached the mortar pit. Sergeant Greely announced that part of the unit would be moving to an outpost location because of some contact in the area, which was some distance from LZ Ike. Sergeant Greely said, "A new mission will be coming up in a few weeks. Your squad will be part of that mission. After it is over, we will have a stand-down and then return to LZ Ike." In the meantime another attack had been in the making, and LZ Ike was hit with another barrage of enemy fire late one evening right before dark. This attack consisted mostly of mortar rounds, which the enemy used as a hit-and-run maneuver. This unsuccessful attack by the enemy set off an atmosphere like the one that had been attempted previously. There seemed to be an increase in rockets and RPGs. That made this attack intense. The mortar was manned in a matter of seconds while I was already out in the mortar pit with Scott. It woke up Jason and Ishmal, who had just started to settle into the hooch after they had just completed a shift. I was unsure of how Ishmal would react because I had never seen him in a battle.

The first thing Ishmal grabbed was his M.16. I told him to just keep the weapon near him for now until the time came for him to use it. But for now, we had to concentrate on the operation of the mortar, which was of immediate concern. I yelled out, "I want you all to get down low and start getting those rounds ready." I took over the helm of the mortar. I was not going to let anybody use the mortar until I had gained confidence in my men. To initiate the rounds going out was very important to me.

I wanted to put down that initial base of fire power. Eventually I would let Jason or Scott get on the mortar once the rounds were steadily being fed to the tube so that I was able to help Ishmal in pulling charges off the .81-millimeter rounds. I knew it had to be an efficient operation, and everybody had to be on the same page. I could see that Ishmal was nervous, so I told him to calm down and just think about what he was doing as he fumbled a couple of rounds, getting them off the stack of rounds.

The enemy targets looked like they were within a three-mile radius. I told the mortar crew the mortar had to be calibrated within that distance. The rounds would have to be walked up and down according to the flashes that were seen from the enemy out in the distance. There needed to be some more adjustments made on the mortar. To not take the proper amount of charges off the rounds could be a deadly mistake because you don't want to put those rounds on top of your people.

That was why I had to help Ishmal to get the proper charges off the rounds. This attack seemed more out of harassment than anything else, but it was the mortar crew's job to stop the attacks and not let them get any closer. Anxiety displayed the sweat that had gotten built up on Ishmal's face and body. He didn't appear to be the strong man he had claimed to be, but he did appear to be a man in desperation to learn what it is to fight in a mortar crew.

This attack was an onslaught of an enemy who tried to proclaim the takeover of LZ Ike or destroy it by an over run, which had happened to other American units. The determination to not let this happen by the soldiers of LZ Ike was still very prevalent. If my mortar squad had anything to do with it, a takeover was not going to happen. Echo Company was going to hold its own. This was a battle for the enemy not to win.

The workings of the mortar platoon along with the perimeter guns, including artillery and light arms, would be in concert with each other as these attacks took place. One thing these attacks was starting to do was take its toll on the adrenaline that I expended on my part because it was the exasperation that I had to keep up to not let my squad down. I began to feel more like I was getting short. The enemy did not want to give LZ Ike any slack.

The battle soon ended with another retreat of the enemy, who still was using evasive tactics that it felt somehow would work. When the dust settled, I saw a Catholic Mass that took place near the headquarters bunker. About eight soldiers were receiving communion. I had only seen this priest once before, but it was rare to see a religious man of the cloth out in the field. Now was definitely the time to give reverence to God.

I went over to where the soldiers were receiving communion and stood in line. I just wanted to continue to be saved in the field of battle. I waited my turn to receive communion. There was a small table that stood near the priest. On the table, I saw a little box with small plastic necklace crosses attached to a small rope to be worn around your neck. I went over to pick out one and put it around my neck as I went back to stand in line. I approached the priest; he laid the small flattened bread on my tongue and blessed me.

The time had come for part of Echo Company to go to the outpost that had been talked about; also, at the same time, Ishmal was leaving for R & R. I didn't know how he got an R & R so early, but somehow he had gotten it. I was relieved that he would be going because he still would do his disappearing acts from time to time. I pictured him doing his Muslim prayers, which I never witnessed him doing. Maybe because he was an American citizen now, his saying of prayers had somehow changed. All I knew was that he thought he was some kind of a playboy from the Arab world who moved into the United States. I always wondered why he would always complain about being in the U.S. Army and not be able to fight for his country in Israel.

Echo Company would continue to do patrols again for a temporary time along with outpost, which would be used to prep and see if the enemy was in a specific area. The outpost would be set on top of a hill with very little cover. I knew that my squad would have to fill a lot of sand bags to get our position fortified. Captain Wright wanted the mortar platoon to make a presence that would counter the Vietcong if they were trying to bring supplies through this area. Scott and Jason were still learning the ropes of how a mortar squad operated, but I continued to notice how they started to become a little lax because maybe they felt this area was a little remote or less hostile, which I felt was not the case at all.

There was still something suspicious about Ishmal. I just couldn't quite put my finger on it; all I wanted Ishmal to do was fight when the time came and be ready to help. The day the unit moved, Ishmal would be on a helicopter on his way to Hong Kong. I wanted to hold off from taking an R & R until the time was right. That evening, the unit arrived on the top of the hill. There was the necessary mortar equipment and other supplies that were needed. The sand bags and pallets were also important because they were used in building our fortification. I knew that it was always important to have a good defensive position, especially if you didn't want your squad out in the open. The first thing that had to be done was get the mortar set up and ready to go. I took on the responsibility to get the mortar squad ready with the help of Jason and Scott. They helped put up the make shift tent that we had bought, along until the hooch could be completed.

The platoon was expecting more supplies so that their position could be more secured. The sand bags needed to be filled so that the squad and the mortar could be protected more as we would fill them throughout the day. I didn't like the idea of sitting up on a hill out in the open. It was the idea of being protected sooner rather than later. The captain was the one who got his position set up first, then the enlisted men followed. Sergeant Greely and the first sergeant got their sleeping quarters in order themselves.

The company commander's tent was set up behind my mortar pit. Days would pass as supplies trickled in. One day, a helicopter with supplies and personnel flew in. The one soldier that got off was Ishmal. It was like he was coming to the unit for the very first time all over again. His fatigues almost looked the same. You could tell that he had been on R & R by the broad smile on his face. I noticed that he was clinging to his ruck sack along with his M.16 as he came to the not-quite-finished mortar pit.

It was the same old devious grin that Ishmal displayed when I first met him. The first thing he said to me was, "The R & R was all right, the women were beautiful. I had a great time! You should have come with me!" I responded, "I'll be going on R & R soon enough. So don't worry." Ishmal was up to his old tricks again, playing hide-and-seek. Jason and Scott were told that some more sand bags needed to be filled. In reluctance, they would fill the sand bags. The hooch was almost built; it needed another layer of sand bags to complete it. The mortar was in place with about fifty mortar rounds ready to go at any time. I worked in earnest around the mortar pit, trying to fill as many bags as I could. I wanted Ishmal to help fill some sand bags, but he was nowhere to be seen. I looked in the hooch to see if I could find him there. I crawled inside the hooch.

This time I found Ishmal crouched down, looking through his ruck sack. I wondered what he was doing. Ishmal turned around. He was startled. Ishmal had a big plastic bag full of marijuana, which looked liked it was fresh from the field. I was stunned. I went over and grabbed him by the shirt and said, "What the hell do you think you're doing!" Ishmal dropped the bag as I held on to his shirt. "This is a combat area! Are you crazy! I ought to beat your fucking ass! Now get the fuck out of here and help fill some sand bags."

He nervously put the bag of marijuana back in his rucksack. His response as he kneeled down in the hooch was, "Oh, I'm just holding this for somebody. I'm not going to smoke it. He back handed me with his fist in a shocked attack. I responded with a show of force as I gave him a right cross while we were both on our knees in the hooch.

He got a pretty good beating from me as we both became exhausted from the fight. I said to him, "Do you want to be charged with an Article 15?" Ishmal replied, "Calm down, I'm not going to let anybody see me with this." I turned and crawled out of the hooch. I was angry as I attempted to calm down from what had just happened.

While Ishmal was inside the mortar pit filling a sand bag, I saw him collaborating with Scott and Jason while they filled their bags as they looked at me. My disgust toward Ishmal was still present as I grimaced at all three men while I filled sand bags and began to wipe down the mortar. The incident was far from over.

The next evening, I was called to the captain's hooch. The captain's name was Wright. I had very little contact with this captain because he was new to the company. My contact would be mostly with NCOs or what you would call noncommissioned officers. To communicate with the noncommissioned officers is what I preferred. For one thing, I never really saw officers engaged in combat. Their duty was to give the troops information about possible enemy locations through communication with other companies back in the rear. I entered the captain's hooch with trepidation; I knew I wasn't there to get slapped on the back. The captain sat on his cot with his back turned to me, smoking a pipe. Then I said, "Hey, Captain, I heard you wanted to see me." The captain turned around in his cot. I stood at attention.

The first thing that came out of the captain's mouth was, "At ease, soldier. I've heard a few things about you, sergeant Durham." While I looked at Captain Wright, he reminded me of Clark Kent, who was Superman on television, except he was a little slimmer; it also complimented him because he was from West Point. He had dark hair and a keener face. The captain took the pipe out of his mouth as he blew out some smoke. The captain then said, "Someone has told me that they smelled marijuana coming from your mortar area. Do you know anything about this, Sergeant Durham?" My answer was, "No, sir! I wouldn't allow anybody to have marijuana in my squad, sir." Then Captain Wright said, "Well, what I'm going to do is relieve you of your duties as squad leader."

I was stunned. The first thing that came to my mind was Ishmal. Then Captain Wright said, "What I'm going to do for now is reduce your stripes to specialist, which is going to be a half stripe taken from you. The necessary paperwork will have to be done to continue the procedure. I just can't have this in my company. What do you have to say for yourself?" I thought a minute and then responded, "You've made a mistake, Captain; I wouldn't allow that kind of activity in my squad. I care about my men. I will have to protest this. I'll write to President Nixon and have him look into this matter. I'm innocent! Another thing since you are going to take my squad, I'll move to the gunner position, where I feel safe."

Then the captain said, "You're dismissed." It seemed like a part of my heart had been ripped out. I wanted revenge but knew now was not the time to get irate, so I did what I told the captain to keep my composure. It was not long after and we were hit by some incoming. I held off the enemy once again with the same tenacity that I displayed in previous battles. I also continued to play my role as the leader as far as I was concerned because nothing was official about a stripe being taken away. I had to bide my time to deal with the situation at hand. My experience was being displayed. I still outranked everyone in the squad and continued to play my role as a squad leader.

As the battle continued, Ishmal contributed with his measured resistance not too far away from being a coward but close enough. He shook to no end as he got mortar rounds ready. There still was disdain in my heart for Ishmal because he betrayed me. Ishmal still had to be prompted to fight along with his cohorts who were a part of the squad. I knew that mutiny could be dangerous when dealing with the enemy, so the best thing for me to do was to stay focused on the mission of getting back home.

The squad would still rely on me as the gunner. This attack was an uphill battle, so the enemy had to be fired down upon relentlessly until there was no fight left in him. The mortars played a key role in pushing the Vietnamese army back once again. This was another attack that was short-lived by the enemy. I knew it was not my nature to give up and that I would continue to fight with the tenaciousness that was still in me.

The mission up on the hill was over. The mortar platoon would move on to a new location where possibly we would get a break from the fighting. This undisclosed area was still somewhere not far from Saigon, which I assumed by guessing from hearing conversation between Sergeant Greely and Top. It still was in the vicinity where the civilians were able to interact with the troops. This new area was located near a river, which had a small set of barracks set up on a bank. To look at a river out in front was something different. Most of the barracks had little screen doors that were their entrances to average-size rooms, which were big enough for about five men. This facility looked like it had been used before by other troops.

There were bunks in the facility that were made out of the wall, which looked kind of odd to me. Captain Wright felt that this location would do for now because we weren't going to be here that long. I started to feel down hearted because of the incident that happened up on the hill. The sooner we'd leave this place, the better I would feel. I started to feel the need for a woman again. I saw Leea's face in a dream one night. I woke up in an abrupt manner. It seemed like it wasn't that long ago that me and Leea were together. I was disgusted about my squad being taken away and being accused of something I didn't do.

There was a Vietnamese family that had a make shift hut made out of plywood along the river bank. It almost looked similar to the barracks we stayed in, except this structure was along the bank of the river about three hundred yards from where the troops stayed. We were told to carry weapons everywhere we went in this area and to travel in groups armed. I wanted to keep my distance from Ishmal. He lived in the barrack next to the one I stayed in. When we encountered each other, we would look the other way, or when we looked at each other, we would grimace.

Sergeant Gregory made an appearance one morning. He knocked on the door. I got off my bunk in a daze from sleep as I wiped my eyes. He asked, "Is Durham in there?" I knew it was him right away. I said, "Yeah it's me, Top, come on in." He looked every bit of the tall red headed soldier he was. He was still the slightly overweight Georgia gentleman that he was. Sergeant Gregory stepped into the wooden compartment. He said, "I heard they took your squad away from you for some bullshit."

"Yes, sir, they took it away."

"Why did they do something like that!"

"I really don't know. I didn't do anything, Top."

"Do you know that you are one of the best soldiers in this outfit? They had no right to do what they did, and I'm going to get to the bottom of this, so just be patient, son." The next thing I knew was that Top turned around and walked out of the door. I got my gear together and decided to take a walk with a few other soldiers.

There had been a few new replacements that had just joined up with Echo Company. I didn't know any of them. There was one new black soldier that I did notice. He was a slender build. He wore a neat-looking boonie cap. He seemed as if he were fun loving and liked to joke. While walking along the river, I noticed the new soldier was involved with the Vietnamese family that lived on the bank of the river.

You would see them as they fished together, but what I noticed the most was that this new soldier found himself a lady friend. She looked like she was the daughter of the family because there was only mama and papasan along with the girl. This relationship between the new soldier and the young Vietnamese girl seemed like it might have been a serious relationship that started to take place. I and a few other troops noticed this event while it was going on. I and the troops I was with decided to take a walk to a concession stand that they had heard about from other troopers. One of the soldiers in the group was named Jack, and he was carrying an automatic pump shotgun. I didn't know where he got the weapon from. I had my M.16 along with the other soldiers that were with us. As we walked down a road, there was a wide open field that we noticed. It caught everybody's attention because of the opening that made the field look like a rifle range.

Jack said, "Come on, there's a clearing over there, let's get some target practice in." I was hesitant about firing a weapon around a civilian area as I thought this was a safe area. We approached the area with caution to make sure it was clear. I then said, "Let me see that shotgun." There was some movement in some brush to our left. I said, "I hear something over in that brush over there." Jack handed the weapon to me. I gave my M.16 to Jack. I walked out farther ahead of the men where I thought I heard the movement.

Somehow the shotgun slipped from my hand and engaged; as soon as it hit the ground, the shells went. The gun began to spin around in a circle. A monkey ran out from the brush that I had concentrated on. The only thing I knew to do was to jump rope until the rounds were expended. The other soldiers ducked behind trees. The rounds bounced off trees, missing them. The weapon soon stopped its movement while I stopped jumping. The other troops began to laugh at me.

I said, "Let's get out of here!" We continued on our journey to find the concession stand that we had heard about. We wanted to get a soda or something to quench our thirst. Around the concession stand was a group of Vietnamese civilians. There were some women in the group who looked at us as we approached. I noticed a made-up store front, which looked like the concession stand that soldiers stood around and talked while they got refreshments. I walked toward the concession stand. A Vietnamese woman stood in front of the concession stand, taking money when she got a soda from the papasan behind the stand.

A small motorcycle with a slender black soldier riding on the back with a Vietnamese woman driver appeared. The black soldier jumped off the bike with his M.16 grasped in his hand and ran over to a Vietnamese woman who stood near me. The next thing I knew was that this soldier swung his M.16 at the woman with the butt end of the weapon. The hit was so hard that it made the woman stagger back, hitting the ground. The slender black soldier with the black band on his wrist shouted at the woman. He said, "Bitch! If you ever do that again, I'll kill you." She cowered down, begging not to be hit again in her Vietnamese language, begging for her life.

There was another commotion that was going on. A line of about eight American soldiers stood in line down a trail that was to the left of the concession stand about fifty yards away. One of the soldiers yelled out, "Hey, guys, come on over here! We got lips! She's giving up some head." The soldier was talking about a Vietnamese woman doing oral sex. I had never experienced having oral sex. Maybe this was the last chance to get the act done before I died. I felt at this time I didn't have anything to lose. The line was moving quickly as the soldiers stood in it waiting for their turn. I was the last one to join the line of soldiers. It wouldn't be long before I had my turn.

The woman begged for her life. The soldiers continued to taunt her. I soon got my turn. When I got in front of the woman, I noticed she had on an orange blouse with black pajamas. She was on her knees. The erection of my penis had begun. I proceeded to pull my fatigue pants down while I pointed my M.16 at the woman's temple. She continued to plea for her life. I looked behind to see what was going on as the rest of the soldiers departed.

The rather attractive Vietnamese woman pleaded once again, "Please don't kill me! Please don't kill me." The woman then proceeded to give me a blow job. I had never experienced a feeling like that before. The M.16 never moved from the woman's temple. She would stop and plead once again, "Please don't tell my sister, please don't tell my sister, she work at the PX, she come by every morning over the bridge." She said, "Please, please, don't let her know." I replied, "I don' give a fuck about your sister!" I decided I wanted to have intercourse with the woman. An American helicopter appeared and hovered over head. The helicopter hovered over us until the act was done.

Later on that evening, I and a few other soldiers went down to the hut that was on the bank of the river to see exactly what was going on with the Vietnamese family on the river. We approached the small hut with weapons in hand. I could see the smoke from something cooking just inside the entrance of the hut. Everybody was squatting down in a small area of the hut, which appeared to be basically one room that included small cooking apparatus and boards to sit on.

Everything was conducive to their lifestyle. There was mamasan, papasan, along with private Lewis, the new black soldier to our unit. Lewis sat next to the young Vietnamese girl while papasan and mamasan were attending a pot of noodles that they were cooking under what appeared to be a fire from c4. There was another thing that I noticed, and that was a television on a small bench, which was hooked up to a small generator.

You could hear the small buzzing sound. It was a television in Vietnamese language. This was something that I really didn't expect to see. I spoke to the new soldier and said, "Hey, what's your name?" The soldier put his arm around the young Vietnamese girl as he gave a big smile and said, "My name's Lewis, and I'm from St. Louis."

"Oh, so you from the see-me state."

"Oh, you mean the show-me state." We both laughed.

CHAPTER 13

REST AND REVOLT

Something came on the TV caught my attention and the rest of us that were there. It looked like some kind of theater play that was being dramatized by Vietnamese actors along with American troops who also appeared to be actors. The American troops sat around campfire, smoking marijuana. The smoke from the fire billowed up. They laughed and joked with one another when all of a sudden, they were surrounded by Vietcong sneaking up behind them and slashing their throats. The Americans were caught by surprise.

The Vietcong then took their weapons and disappeared in the dark. I couldn't believe what I saw right before my eyes. There was a jolt of shock that went throughout my body. The family seemed undisturbed by the event that had just taken place. Private Lewis continued to be affectionate to the young girl he met. It was almost as if he was dating her. On that note, I decided to leave the premises.

Lewis decided that his fate would be with this Vietnamese family he met. His love for the young Vietnamese girl showed through and through as if he had been mesmerized into a state of unconsciousness. It became apparent; he wasn't going to leave any time soon. The next day, Echo Company headed back to LZ Ike. The little stand-down was over. Private Lewis missed movement to be seen no more. He would be absent without leave. Landing Zone Ike still took on the look of ruggedness that it possessed. I was not happy being in the status of not having a squad. My gunner position was still in my hands, which made me feel a little more comfortable. The uneasiness of not being a squad leader troubled me. My mood was to just focus on operating the mortar. The guard watch was set up to ensure that I would have the watch in the wee hours of the night, right before sun rise. There were times when Jesse, the medic, would make rounds with his bag of medical supplies, being ready to aid the troops if he needed to. I watched Jesse as he laid his medicine bag near his hooch. He went inside his hooch for the night. It was a star-filled night as I stared into the darkness around me. The intense conscious glare engulfed me. I felt more depressed than ever. I stared at the medicine bag that lay outside Jesse's hooch. I looked around to see if anybody would notice me as I jumped from the mortar pit to get to the bag.

At this point, I didn't care. I reached for the bag and began to go through it. I felt around for the pills. I located the pills and grabbed a handful. I could see the pills from the moon of the sky. They were yellow and orange. I was soon back inside the mortar pit. Before I realized it, I swallowed about twenty pills down my throat. The pills were followed by a gulp of water from my canteen. In a matter of minutes, I felt like I was going unconscious as everything appeared blurred. I became dizzy. Everything seemed like it was off balance. I staggered around the mortar pit. The pills took away my equilibrium.

This situation put me in a panicked state. I was out of control. All of a sudden, vulnerability set in. I continued to stagger but still realized where the mortar was. I didn't want to knock it down because of my awkwardness. The drunkenness from the pills wouldn't let me go as I still stumbled around the pit. I got on my knees and started praying. *Help me, God, for I know not what I do!* I soon noticed the blurriness clear and my composure come back. The pills stopped taking effect as I got back to my conscious state once again. I got up from my knees and walked around the pit and said, "Thank you, God. You spared my life."

All of a sudden, a whistling sound of explosions started making their presence inside the perimeter. I quickly grabbed my steel pot and flight vest. I yelled out, "Incoming! Incoming! Incoming! Incoming!" Scott was the first one to appear out of the hooch. He yelled back into the hooch, repeating what I had already said. My mortar squad responded and began getting in their proper positions to get the rounds out. The rounds that came in were rockets and RPGs with their distinct sounds as they passed overhead, hitting inside the perimeter.

I spotted the flashes, where they were set off in the wood line. The flashes were coming from the west, so I had to make the proper adjustments and swing the mortar in that direction. In a matter of seconds, the .81-millimeter rounds were going out of the tube. This time, the reflexes of the squad had gotten better.

Our outgoing fire was being countered by the enemy rounds as they got close to our sleeping quarters. Jesse was still inside his hooch.

A round from a rocket landed right on top of Jess's hooch. It was a direct hit. The .50 and .60 machine guns made short burst because they weren't sure how close the enemy was in the wood line. The shadows in the woods were being seen. Someone yelled out, "Gooks in the wire!" Joe lit up the razor wire with the .50-caliber machine gun as it made its mark where the enemy was trying to come into the perimeter. Claymores continued to go off as the heat, dust, and shrapnel were seen in the midst of the smoke and smolder.

Our .81-millimeter rounds dwindled down as the mortar countered the enemies attack. It was the same relentlessness that I began to exert with all the power I had, along with pushing the squad to continue to do its thing. I could glimpse the flashes once again along the wood line as I continued to man the mortar, directing accurate fire on the enemy positions. I continued to tell my squad the amount of charges that needed to be taken off the rounds as I stood next to the mortar, dropping rounds into the mortar tube, directing the rounds.

Ishmal was crawling around the mortar pit, looking for his M.16, saying as he yelled out, "Where's my M.16!" I said, "Don't worry about your M.16, we need to get these rounds out." Scott found Ishmal's M.16 and threw it to him. He soon started helping with the rounds. Scott and Jason were the ones giving the most help as Ishmal slowly crawled to the location of the mortar rounds. I heard the impact of the .81-millimeter rounds along the wood line that were not being wasted. The blunt impacts were making their marks. Beehive rounds from the artillery started to make their impression as they burst inside the wood line. I could hear them being launched from an artillery crew that was just to the back of my mortar pit. The sound of the men deploying the rounds in the artillery station was close. The artillery rounds were being sent out relentlessly. Soon the incoming faded as Sergeant Greely said, "Cease fire! Cease fire!"

The command was soon heeded as the flares' illuminations dropped to the ground. Then there came the appearance of the gunships making their entrance, showing more fire power. The streams of red bullets were seen coming from their guns along the wood line. It was almost like looking at a laser show as hundreds and thousands of bullets streamed from the ships in the sky. I could see resistance as rounds started going up toward the helicopters. The *kak, kak, kak* sound of the AK-47 rounds were seen and heard trying to reach the helicopters. Soon the helicopters released all of their rounds and were headed back to their base.

The resistance finally stopped as the sun rose. I could see the sun crack through the trees in the east. Day appeared while the enemy retreated. The dust settled once again, and the assessment of damage was viewed. The medics took some of the wounded and dead down to the helicopter pad to be taken out of the area. Sergeant Greely made his appearance from the bunker that was to the right of the mortar pit. The first thing he said was, "Is everybody all right?" No one responded. Then someone yelled out, "Doc's hooch got hit!"

Sergeant Greely went over to the hooch that was demolished. He saw the colorful M.16 that Jesse possessed still intact. He discovered Jesse's mangled body. "We're going to need a body bag over here. There's a man over here that needs to be put in one." The medics came over with a stretcher and began doing their duty while some of the other troops walked around and picked up body parts.

I looked further out into the smoldering and dusty environment, along with the bodies of dead Vietnamese who were scattered inside and outside the perimeter. The attack was foiled once again. The impression that it gave to me was when was this going to end? The soldier that was the contentious objector and carried a flower-covered and painted M.16 was zipped up in the body bag. The reprieve would be short-lived. The clean up was continual as the operation of the landing zone was in some order as soldiers continued to fill body bags. I rubbed my nose as the stench became part of my fatigues along with the dirt. It would linger in the air as days went on.

Sergeant Greely made an announcement; he said, "I have a few slots open for in-country R & R's. We need these to be filled for Vung Tau." He pointed to me and said, "I know you haven't been on an R & R yet, Durham, so now is your chance." It couldn't have happened at the right time for me. I still reeled from the last attack and the idea of my squad being taken away. I looked at it as an opportunity to cool off. "I'm ready to go, Sarge!"

"Get your gear together because there's a chopper coming in to take you to Vung Tau about 0600, so be ready because you're going to leave as you are." I managed to get some clean fatigues that were washed while I took a quick shower. I got some of the battle dirt off my body. The relief was needed. Now all I needed was to find a woman for the three brief days being away from the action.

It was just before dark when the helicopter approached what appeared to be a small mountainous region right up against the ocean, which seemed to have its back to Vietnam. This added to the look of the oasis. It was set up on a plateau as a village that was out of nowhere. The helicopter approached the destination; I could see the presence of the military installation. As the helicopter maneuvered its way into the large compound, it was surrounded by a perimeter. The heat from the engine of the helicopter felt a little uncomfortable as the sun started to set. I looked over at the helicopter crew and gave them a thumbs-up as they made their approach over the towered security that was set up. The gunners never took their hands off the .60s as their grip got tighter. The helicopter hovered over the man-made airfield. This was the backdrop for the large village of Vung Tau.

Vung Tau was just beyond the perimeter. The helicopter landed. I managed to jump off the helicopter. I had to check in at the entrance of the compound, which was the pass-through point to Vung Tau. The American guard that was at the gate told me that I would have to leave all my equipment at the entrance before going into Vung Tau, including my M.16. I was not too happy about leaving my M.16 behind. I told the MP, "How would you like to be unarmed? I'm naked, man. You sure this is the right thing for me to do?"

The MP said, "Don't worry, I got your back." The MP at the gate directed me to a small installation where I was able to sleep overnight. The direction the MP sent me was about one-half mile into Vung Tau; as nightfall came, I began to walk and look around. I was uncomfortable as I looked around at the darkened, gray-shaded buildings in the dark of the night. The full moon was my company on this night in an unknown village that looked as threatening as being out in the field. People would pass by me and turn their faces as if they didn't want to know who I was.

They appeared to be Vietnamese as I tried to blend into the environment. This castaway place seemed like it could be a haven for the enemy. My approach was with caution as I walked through the streets of Vung Tau. Soon I came to my destination. It was a Red Cross station. Another MP was at the entrance of the building, which appeared to be a small boarding house. It was like a way station for soldiers to stay at night. I found a small room to myself. Troops were coming in and out. They would stay there for a little and soon would go back to their units when their stay ended.

It seemed to be that all was on my mind was getting laid. The sooner this would happen, the better I would feel. The following morning I was able to get breakfast or fruit from the Red Cross station. There was no time to waste, so I was on my way to the main village. These few days would go by quickly. The day had turned out to be sunny. I got to see what Vung Tau was like during the daylight hours. I should have brought a camera but realized this wasn't a vacation like back in the states. To me, it just was a period for me to get out of the field and hope that my life would not be in danger. It was a time for me to really feel good about myself because I was still alive. I needed something to lift up my confidence and get over the paranoia that haunted me in Vung Tau.

I wanted to get the loss of my squad off my mind for my brief stay in Vung Tau. That issue would be dealt with when the time would come. The first thing I did was find out where a woman was to spend the night with until it was time to go back to the field. The exchange of money would have to do. I had about thirty dollars in Vietnamese money to get me what I wanted. This was a time I needed someone to comfort me.

A rendezvous with a woman would have to take place somewhere. I found a trail to venture on as I walked through Vung Tau. I saw a blond American soldier with his boonie cap dangling from the back of his neck. He was buying some trinkets from a papasan along the road. I walked toward the U.S. soldier, who looked like he had been in the area for a little while. I tapped the soldier on his shoulder and said, "Hey man, where can a soldier get a drink from around here?" The soldier turned around as if he were glad to hear an American voice. I noticed a bad scar across his cheek. He said, "Hey! How you doing, brother? What are you doing up here? Are you on R & R or something?"

"Yeah, I'm on R & R and looking for some place to relax, brother. Do you know of any place around here where I can get a drink?" I looked at the military patch on the soldier's fatigues. It was from the Big Red One. He gave the papasan some money as he got his souvenir elephant.

"Yeah, I know a place you can go if you're looking for a few drinks." He pointed to a trail that was winding up to the top of a hill. "You see the top of that hill off to your right? There is a club called the Tiger Club that has a bar and some women. They might be able to help you out. I'm ready to get the fuck back to my unit. I've been here long enough. You can have this place. I'm ready to get out of here. I'm starting to get short, and I'll be going home for good, if you know what I mean. I've been hit once, and I don't want to be hit again. I'm healed now, so I can go back to my unit."

"Hey, you're not by yourself. I'm starting to get short too."

"Hey that's all right, man. Watch out for the gooks. They're all over this place." I looked around and saw the villagers, who seemed to be friendly as they pedaled there goods and went about their daily business in Vung Tau. "I guess I'll go find that club you're talking about." I walked away and went in the direction the soldier had pointed out.

I passed by various Vietnamese people who made me suspicious as some of the Vietnamese men looked me up and down. They had that rugged look as if they had been in the field. Some of them were on bikes, carrying objects in burlap bags on their shoulders. Some carried water and vegetable items and other food on their heads. They seemed harmless, but they were enemies in disguise to me. I wanted to blend in the crowd as much as possible.

The people that lived up in this mountain village seemed as if they weren't a part of the war that was going on outside their region. While

I walked up the trail, I noticed a tall young black-looking male who had a large red Afro that made him stand out among the villagers. He was moving a bicycle down the trail with a basket on it. He was dressed in Vietnamese garb. I finished the walk up the trail to the hill. I walked up to a huge tree. It had steps winding up to a large tree house built on top of a large trunk. The steps led up to a large room. It was like nothing that I had seen before. It was a marvel that men could build something like this in the middle of nowhere.

The stairs ended as I stood on a platform. I looked down toward the second floor of the structure, which had a sign that was across the top that said Tiger Club. I stood at the entrance. This was a huge club. I looked down the stairwell to the left, which was where the bar was located. The bar covered the entire left side of the floor, which had about twenty bar stools and scores of different kinds of alcoholic beverages in the background on the back shelves.

A cash register was located in the middle of the bar, along with an older Vietnamese woman who acted as a host while taking orders from the barmaids. There were also implanted bamboo trees that were strewn throughout the floor in front of the bar, which gave it an exotic look. I walked down the staircase to the bar and saw American soldiers sitting at various tables that were on the floor. While I approached the bar, a couple of Vietnamese women of the night approached me in a suggestive manner as they grabbed at my crotch. They said, "Hey, GI, do you want woman tonight?" They followed me to the bar and stood around me as they talked to one another. All I wanted to do was have a seat at the bar so I could decide what kind of drink I wanted. The women departed and greeted other soldiers that were coming down the stairs.

The older-looking Vietnamese bartender that was behind the bar had a white blouse on along with black pajamas and the straw hat that they regularly wore. This woman had a chin strap on her hat as she smiled with part of her black teeth. She set out a napkin and spoke in broken English. She said, "GI, want drink?" I said, "I'll have a coke!" It was kind of early in the day for me to have alcohol, so I decided that I would nurse my cokes for the remainder of the afternoon while I gazed around the bar. There were five cokes lined up in front of me. I went back and forth to piss in a hole that was located in a back room. As I walked by, women would still grab at my crotch to get attention.

Now was time for me to make my move. I noticed to my left, there was another stairway that led down to a seating area with tables and a small bar to the side. There was one table that I noticed in the middle of this particular area that had a woman who sat by herself. I had been glancing over at the attractive Vietnamese woman all afternoon. She didn't have the regular straw hat on but had her hair in a short style, which complemented her Asian face.

She seemed to separate herself from the other women. Her face was a light complexion that was almost white. She also had on a different kind of blouse and skirt on that stood out. I also noticed that she was also nursing a drink. I ordered her a rum and coke. I lifted up my glass to the woman as I pointed to the drink in my hand. This was the signal for me to come over to where she was sitting. She smiled as I sat down with the drinks in my hands. My response was, "How you doing? Do you want a drink?"

She nodded her head in agreement. Then the Vietnamese woman spoke as we gazed at each other. She said in a low voice and broken English, "My name Mia. You look for woman tonight?" I responded, "You boom boom girl? I need a place to sleep tonight." I folded my hands and pretended like I was asleep."

"I have a place to sleep, GI. You want to go? I have surprise for you." She made an effort for me to understand what she was saying as she called a girl over to say some English words. I looked at her and said, "You drink and then we get ready to go."

I rubbed my hand across the side of her face in a smooth manner and said, "You beaucoup number 1! Then I put my hand on her thigh in a suggestive manner. Her face brightened up as I got fresh with her. She gave me a response with an even wider smile to me make me know that she might accommodate me. We finished our drinks. I asked, "Are you ready to go? Where do you live?" She said, "I live in Vung Tau." A smile came on my face. "You're right, you do live in Vung Tau." Then we got up and went toward the door. The darkness made its presence known when we went outside.

The shadowy buildings gave a mystique to the village on the mountain. The walk through the streets of Vung Tau was dicey as we walked through a rough neighborhood, going through alleys and side streets. The silhouette of an AK-47 being exchanged for money caught my eye as two Vietnamese men made the exchange in our presence on the side of a building. Mia took my hand, leading the way to a destination unknown to me. I increased my vigilance around every other corner as Mia got frustrated with me. Then we came upon a building that looked like a little chateau and boarding house. The stairs were narrow as we climbed the side entrance of the building. As we went up the steps, I could see that the blinds were closed as I looked at several windows on the building. We reached the entrance and Mia unlocked the door. She opened the door, and there was a long Oriental rug that was on the floor. I looked up and down the hallway at the wall and saw French pictures and other artifacts that were on little tables in the hallway. Mia opened the door to a room on the left.

We entered the medium-sized room and closed the door. There was a bed in the middle of the room. The bed was encircled with see-through curtains that were pink. It looked like something out of a fairy tale. The exotic-looking bedroom was enticing. Mia closed the door while we were all alone. I pulled Mia toward me in a suggestive manner as she slightly pulled away. I didn't understand what was going on as I became perplexed by her mannerism.

She then said, "Wait here. I'll be right back." She turned her back to me and left the room. I became inquisitive about what was going to happen next. I walked around the room, looking for all possible hiding places. Maybe this was a setup. I was defenseless; there was nothing I could do about it. There I was all alone in this strange room. Mia returned to the room, but this time she was not alone. She came with another young girl who appeared to be of black descent. The beautiful black girl stood there in bewilderment. She looked exotic in her see-through apparel, which set everything off she wore. As the girl stood there with Mia, she kept quiet. Mia motioned to me and said, "She for you. You like?"

"I don't want her. I want you." I pushed the new girl to the side and turned to Mia. I grabbed her shoulders and said, "I want you, not her." I stood between both women as they spoke in Vietnamese. The argument seemed to have swayed to Mia's favor as they both realized what I wanted. Mia looked at the black girl and told her to leave. I put my hands over my head and said, "I can't believe this shit!"

"Why!" The black woman left the room. "I can't believe this shit!" I looked at Mia and gently grabbed her shoulders once again as I saw tears in her eyes. I asked her, "Why you cry?" The Asian woman looked up at me in a melancholy way and said, "They say at night black GI grow tail like a tiger." I reassured her and said as I shook my head, "You were told a lie. I'm not going to grow a tail."

I pulled Mia closer and began to stroke her. She seemed as if she were embarrassed. I gave her a passionate kiss and began to disrobe her. I continued to stroke Mia as I felt her buttocks. My fatigues pants dropped to the floor. She looked down at me as her eyes widened. I walked the Asian woman to the bed. We had intercourse like there was no tomorrow. This evening was the most passionate experience that I had ever had.

The bliss was not interrupted as the sunlight came through the curtains the next morning. Mia slept while I looked in the mirror at my buttocks. I even felt it. I wanted to know if I had grown a tail. I shook her as she lay half-asleep. She looked up at me. I pointed to my buttocks. "Does it look like I have a tail?"

New sergeant stripes were sown on my fatigue shirt in Vung Tau. I picked up my combat gear from the main entrance to Vung Tau and looked back at the village on the mountain. My helicopter waited to take me back out into the combat zone. I secured my M.16 and was ready to go back to LZ Ike with trepidation from the brief rest. The high-octane adrenaline started to flow again as the helicopter lifted off the tarmac headed back to LZ Ike. The next mission was on my mind. I arrived at LZ Ike with no fanfare but with anxiety that I was still attached to the squad that I had left briefly. Jason, Scott, and Ishmal were still a part of the squad.

It seemed the attitudes of Jason, Ishmal, and Scott did not change for the better, but regardless of the way they felt, my status in the squad never changed. There was a rumor that there was a new commanding officer coming to replace the commander that had been there at LZ Ike. The word had spread quickly about this new colonel coming to Landing Zone Ike. Sergeant Greely came over to the mortar pit and said, "Men, we'll be getting a new commander coming in here after dark. I just thought I'd let you know what's up."

I questioned Sergeant Greely, "Is that going to make it any better around here, Sarge? We're still getting hit." Sergeant Greely turned around and walked toward headquarters and said, "I'm going to get briefed about what's going on right now. By the way, his name is commander Stanly." I then yelled back to Sergeant Greely and said, "Sarge, we'll be here waiting." In a laughing manner, I yelled over to Joe. "Joe, did you hear that? Just make sure you got that .50 on rock and roll! I'll take care of my end, so we don't want no half-stepping!" Joe looked over at me and said, "Boy, you crazy! I'm going to have to keep my eye on you!" We both laughed once again.

CHAPTER 14

ON THE WAY HOME

Just as Sergeant Greely told about the new commander's arrival time, the sun had just set. The commander was on his way to the firebase. The helicopters managed to find their way to the helicopter pad at LZ Ike. The helicopters were accompanied with a small entourage. The lead helicopter made its way into LZ Ike's landing zone, with the commander's helicopter leading the way into the perimeter helicopter pad. The commander stepped off his helicopter. I could see the new commander in front of about six soldiers who were along with him. Everybody in the squad was out in the mortar pit as the commander made his presence. The commander passed by Joe's bunker with not much fan fare. I watched as the commander waited for the rest of the soldiers to enter the headquarters bunker.

The Vietcong had got wind to our new commander. A rocket whizzed in over the mortar pit, right on top of the command bunker where the commander stood under the entrance. The sand bags shattered on top of the entrance as the rocket penetrated. RPGs and mortars rounds along with other rockets came after the first round made its mark. The *incoming* words were announced. All hell broke loose. I scrambled in the mortar pit as the incoming mortar rounds continued to penetrate the perimeter. Within about thirty seconds, I said, "Okay, let's get some rounds out!" The men's reactions improved some more as I admonished them to act quickly. The wood line was about a mile out with the presence of Vietcong and NVA. They were well organized in their dispersion of rounds that were being administered. They charged the perimeter with no let up.

It still didn't stop me from getting the necessary rounds out with the speed and accuracy that I was accustomed to. It seemed like the enemy was determined to breach the perimeter. It was not going to happen on my watch. The trip flares illuminated the sky along with the stars and moon, which helped. The rounds impacted inside the perimeter as they hit targets, except for my mortar pit. I turned the mortar to a higher point.

Claymores were going off. Joe opened up on the .50 as if there were no tomorrow. I yelled over to Joe, "Bring smoke, Joe!"

"Don't let them get in!" Joe replied as he handled the gun while it was eating up .50-caliber rounds, which spewed out rounds nonstop. Joe controlled the big gun with a tight grip. He wouldn't let go. A few of the enemies managed to crawl and elude the rounds of the .60 and the .50-caliber machine guns until they got caught in the wire. One Vietnamese soldier who got inside the perimeter ran in a bunker and blew himself up to my far left. I walked the rounds along the edge of the wood line as I saw human images of movement.

I looked back toward headquarters, where it took the direct hit. Part of the structure was still holding up as rockets made their way to try and finish off the structure. Medics came out of the smoke with stretchers of bodies as their names were being called. I saw the new commander emerge as he appeared from out of the headquarters bunker debris. I noticed the commander was bandaged up from head to toe. He had taken an extensive amount of shrapnel. He was wrapped up with bandages that made him look like a mummy. I could see his eyes as he walked around the mortar pit with his .45 in hand, acting like a man who was possessed. He went toward the bunker where Joe was.

With tenacity, he yelled out orders in his pathetic state. He said, "Okay, men, keep the fire power going! We're going to get those bastards, so don't give up, men, keep fighting." His words were being muffled as the sounds of rounds were going out and coming in. His silhouette was very much visible. I steadily kept putting out .81-millimeter rounds as the commander came up behind Joe while he concentrated on getting fire power out with the .50-caliber machine gun. I yelled out, "Joe! Somebody is behind you, Joe!" Joe turned around.

He saw the mummy-type figure coming toward him, whom he had mistaken for the enemy. All he thought about was going into his hand-to-hand mode. This mummy-type figure startled Joe. He thought about his safety. He left the .50-caliber machine gun and commenced to beating up the commander, forgetting about his .50-caliber machine gun as he started beating the commander in a street-fight mode, throwing jabs left and right.

His fists met their mark as the commander staggered from the blows. Joe was ferocious as he pounded on the commander.

It was as if Joe had lost his senses. I yelled out to Joe. "Joe! Joe! Joe! Let him go before you kill him! That's the commander! He's not a gook!" Joe came to his senses. He gathered himself and got back on the .50-caliber machine gun. Joe finally realized this man was not a gook. While the colonel was on the ground, I yelled out, "Medic! Medic! Medic! We need a medic over here!" Sweat soaked through the fatigues of the men as the battle went on. The battle kept up momentum as rounds continually went out. The colonel was put on a litter and moved back to the medics' station. The battle soon subsided as the helicopters began to come in with fire power, along with helping to evacuate the wounded. This had turned out to be quite a battle, which was an attempt to over run the firebase. Firebase Ike lost an incoming commander, who was sent back to the rear in a medevac helicopter. The NVA was determined to take LZ Ike. They wanted to see if its defense could be penetrated. This was not happening. The enemy was losing hundreds of men.

It was the day after while I took a shit in the latrine when Captain Wright entered the makeshift toilet holder. He sat down on one of the man-made shitters that was next to me. As he sat down, I said, "How you doing, Captain?" He said, "I'm doing okay, Durham. Durham, we're going to need another mortar squad. I believe by getting another mortar squad, it will strengthen us a little more on LZ Ike. I want to know if you're interested in having another mortar squad." I looked at him and turned away. I wanted to think for a little while. "Yeah, I'll take a squad under one condition."

"What's the condition, Durham?"

I hesitated to speak again. "I want an all-black squad."

The captain paused for a minute. "Consider it done. You're short, so I want you to go on an out-of-country R & R before you get your squad started. That slot is open because you're next in line to go."

"That sounds good to me. I want to go to Singapore."

To go somewhere different seemed better for me. A lot of the soldiers were going to Hong Kong. Hong Kong was a place where I had no interest in going. By way of Bien Hoa, I would go through the same procedure as if it were going on in-country R & R. This time the C-130 airplane would transport me out of country on my R & R. My military equipment would be left behind once again as I made the transition from Bien Hoa. I pulled sixty dollars out of my pocket. I would be able to get cleaner fatigues. My stay at Bien Hoa would be brief while the various planes kept up their daily activities at the large airport.

The troops at Bien Hoa went to various places in Vietnam as well as throughout the world. This was a trip that I took as a foreign soldier who was there as a tourist instead of a soldier in the country. The plane flight was on a clear day. The plane loaded with troops made its way to the flat-looking, city like town. The buildings were of stucco-looking style. These buildings were close together and some sparsely scattered as I looked at the land below. Singapore took on a rural look as the plane approached the airport.

As the plane landed, I could see the airport was nothing like Bien Hoa. The activity of the Singapore people who worked at the airport was evident. They were diligent at work while the plane rolled into its station. The airport almost looked similar to an American airport. I made my way through the airport to look for a taxi to take me to the town to find me a place to stay. Finding my way through the airport was done with a bit of ease as I walked through it with no fanfare. My main destination was getting to the city. There were several cabs lined up outside the airport. As soon as I got out of the gates to the airport, a short middle-aged cabbie with what appeared to be a torn pilot's cap on his head approached me. He was short with a broad smile and thick mustache. In his unusual voice, he said, "Hey, GI, you look for cab?"

"Yeah! You got a cab that goes to the hotel?"

"Come with me! I show you!"

We approached an old-looking yellow cab, which reminded me of the yellow cabs back in the states. The cab driver opened the passenger's side door. I threw my bag in the back seat. The cab started up with the sputtering sound of the engine. The cab driver quickly made his way through the airport traffic. He knew the route very well. His close brushes with other automobiles made him an expert driver as we made our way out of the airport without an accident.

I looked out of the front window of the cab. I could see the spread-out skyline that was ahead. The cab quickly approached the city. It felt like I was a regular customer instead of a combat soldier who was on leave. The buildings seemed to be well spaced, except for the alleys that were in between. I saw vendors' stands along the walkways of the streets.

People were administrating their trades, which looked like bazaars along the street. People walked by, observing and buying different wares that the sellers were distributing. Soon the cab driver came to a street that had buildings on it that looked like hotels. I wasn't quite sure if these buildings were hotels or not. The cab driver stopped at a cottage-type-looking hotel. The driver pointed and said, "This hotel is for GIs!" I acknowledged what the driver was saying and decided to go ahead and pay him. The cab driver was elated once he received his fare. A big smile was on his face. A sign was hanging from the front of the hotel that said Welcome. I got out of the cab and walked under a canopy, which was into the main entrance to the hotel. The symbols of the foreign language stood out on the hotel. While holding my duffel bag, it entered my mind about how I was going to get around. So I decided to run back to the cab.

The cab I got out of was still idling as if it waited for me. I approached the cab while the driver sat in it, counting his cash. The broad smile was still on his face as he looked up. I managed to communicate to the driver about a need to have a cab for the day. I walked back to the check-in desk. I looked around the foreign hotel lobby briefly to get a glimpse of the artifacts that were from Singapore. The necessary information was given to the desk clerk. The small man behind the desk was dressed as if he were a bell hop and manager at the same time. He seemed to be very precise in his mannerism. All the colors in the room brought out the Oriental look. The man with the black hair and small-rimmed glasses passed the room keys to me.

The number 10 key written in white was handed to me. I paid the bus boy as he pointed in the direction that I needed to go. My room was not that far away as I observed the number on the door that was adjacent to the back of the hotel lobby. The walkway led to the west wing, which was accessible to the lobby of the hotel. The door with the number 10 written on it was opened by the key that I put in it. The first thing I noticed was the bed in the middle of the room. Also on the left side of the bed was a small stand with a telephone on it. There was a dresser and mirror, which was located against the wall in front of the bed. There were also mirrors that flanked all sides of the room and the ceiling. I noticed a closet that was located near the dresser.

A quick assessment was made of the room as I found an area to put my duffel bag. I used the restroom in the room. The cab driver stood by his cab as he continued to smile. I got in the cab. The driver closed my door and went to the driver's side of the car. In his broken English, the driver said, "Where you want to go, GI?" I looked at him and gave him the shape of a coke bottle. Then he saw a woman walking on the street and pointed at her.

The cab driver smiled and looked at me. I nodded my head in agreement. The ride through the Singapore streets was insightful as I noticed the boulevard-type streets that were adjacent to the alleyways. I also noticed the other modes of transportation being used as the people of Singapore traversed across the town.

We soon arrived in an area of houses, which almost looked like hotels. At the same time, these structures looked like houses. The cab driver got out of the cab. He directed me to follow him to a large-style house. We approached the door to the house. The cab driver pointed to the doorbell and said, "You ring bell." I did what he told me. The door bell rang. Soon a woman who almost looked like a mamasan looked through the small drapes that were located on the windowpane of the door. I could see as she opened the door that she was some type of madame. She had on a purple dress, which seemed like night apparel. She almost looked like a gypsy. The cab driver stayed outside as the woman opened the door wider. I gave him his money. I said to the driver, "Wait for me." She pulled me into the house. The inside of the house was dark until the woman began to open some of the blinds. The opened blinds brought light into the house.

The large light purple-type room had but a few small couches and lamps, with a large chandelier in the middle of the big living room. I noticed to the far side on the right, there was a large staircase, which came from a balcony. The woman grabbed my arm again and pulled me almost to the middle of the room.

She spoke in a loud voice as if she were giving instructions to someone. She looked toward the stairwell that was going to the balcony. The woman clapped her hands as a formation of young women started coming down the large staircase. There were thirty women who came down the stairs in all forms and sizes. There was a long rug that was almost in the middle of the room that the women lined up on.

They came to a stop in front of me and the madame. I was stunned as I stood there in front of all these women with various types of clothing on. Their look was appealing as I stared at all of them. The madame turned toward me and said, "You want woman? You pick one and go have some fun! Maybe you fall in love." She smiled at me.

I looked at the madame. The decision would be a hard one for me to make. I looked up and down the line and began to walk down the line in front of the women. I inspected so I would make a good choice. I would touch and turn each one around. Some were almost my height and some were small in stature.

Some would even expose their breast to me. There were a few of them who had small umbrellas that went along with their outfits. They almost looked like models. I walked back to the middle of the line. My eyes got fixed on one girl. She froze me in my tracks. Her face was a round V-shaped face like an Audrey Hepburn. She was kind of short but petite in stature. She had on a short red skirt along with a polka-dot blouse. I pulled her from out of the line and spun her around. I looked at the madame and gave my approval. I said, "This is the one." The madame said, "Her name is Trina."

The madame responded to the woman as she jumped for joy. The madame said, "You pay me for one week!" I then said, "How much?" I want thirty American dollars. I reached in my pocket and gave the proper amount of money to the madame. Once this procedure happened, the girls turned and started heading back up the winding staircase. The transaction was made. Everyone seemed to be pleased as I and the woman smiled and walked out the door. The madame spoke to the girl in her native language as we walked toward the cab. The driver was waiting as he opened the door to the cab. The arrival back at the hotel was pleasant as I caressed the woman in my arms. I attempted to speak with the woman, using gestures and broken English that I had gotten accustomed to while being in Southeast Asia.

The first thing I wanted to do once we got to the hotel room was call back to the states. I picked up the phone on the dresser. A radio was on the dresser. I turned the knob on the radio. The radio station was playing a gospel song called "Oh Happy Day," which I was feeling being away from the chaos of the battlefield. The woman undressed me to get me more into the mood. The operator had gotten through, and my mother answered the phone. She said, "Hello!" I answered, "Hello, Mom!" Her voice got higher as she replied, "Hi, Junior, I'm so glad to hear from you. How are you doing?"

"I'm doing okay now, Mom! I'm not in the field! I'm on R & R in Singapore!" She said, "Oh, you are. I'm so glad to hear your voice! Are you taking care of yourself?"

"I'm doing okay, Mom. I'm at a hotel here in Singapore, and I'm here with a woman!"

She responded, "Oh yeah! It's just so good hearing from you!"

My mother continued to talk. "Everybody here is doing fine and waiting for you to return. I don't want to talk too long because you'll have a high phone bill."

"Hopefully, I'll be home soon with the help of God. I have to go now, Mom." The woman started to stroke me as she finished taking off my clothes.

With all the excitement, I told my mother good-bye and hung up the phone. The option was not coming out of the room for air because this was an experience that I wanted to enjoy to the utmost of my being. I managed to get out of the room one day because the girl named Trina wanted to go to where she lived to get another change of clothes. I also wanted to go shop to get a couple of suits made. I needed to get out of the room and get some air from all the extracurricular activity.

The clothing store included tables of different kinds of Asian cloth material, including silk. Cloth was scattered and spread on the floor of the shop. There were also a couple of sewing machines that were in the back of the shop. I got measured as Trina looked on at the shopkeeper who was small in stature and with some kind of green cap over his head. I picked out two sets of gray material. Trina said, "Looks good!" She smiled and shook her head up and down. We inspected the material as the tailor looked on.

Trina took me to where she lived, which didn't look that much different from the hotel that we stayed in. Trina lived up on the second floor of the hotel-type complex. The room was brightly lit and colored as the sun shone in through the window. The window faced the left side of the room, with a dresser right under the window. The bed was located to the side with a bunch of teddy bears on it. The bed had a pink spread on it.

Trina went to her closet, which was full of clothes. She picked through the clothes, and then she walked from the closet over to the dresser. One of the first things she showed me were three stacks of pictures that stood about a foot tall. She proudly displayed these pictures of military men as if they were trophies. She picked some of them up and showed them to me. These pictures of soldiers she had been with made my heart sink. I was just a statistic.

Trina said, "You see, GIs treat me good!" She smiled with pleasure as she continued to show the pictures to me. She walked over to the closet to find the clothes she needed for the day. I felt like I was two-feet tall. It had come to a point where I felt it was time to get on with the rest of my tour of duty. The idea of getting out of Singapore couldn't have come at a better time.

On the plane going back to Bien Hoa, I was not my normal self. A slight chill had come over my body. An extra amount of sweat came from my face. Once the plane landed, I wanted to find the latrine. There was a latrine I noticed near the main compound of Bien Hoa.

There was a stinging sensation in my penis when I urinated in the trough. I looked down at my penis. A notice of discharge came along with the pain. The irritation made me feel weak. It was time for me to get to a medic. There was not going to be any chance of me going back out in the field in this type of condition. I yelled out to a medic who walked by me.

I explained what was going on to the medic. The medic led me to a medical tent that was not far away from the latrine. It was a big green tent with the Red Cross patch on it. It was just on the edge of the flight line near some bunkers on the edge of the perimeter, well protected by rows of .60 machine guns perched up on bunkers, which were fortified with about five layers of barbed wire set out about a good quarter of a mile out. I walked into the tent. A medic was working on a wounded soldier. I walked over to him to get his attention. Another medic who seemed like he was stationed there approached me.

He said, "What can I do for you, soldier?" I said in a strained voice, "Something's wrong with me, Doc." The medic looked at me. A grimace was on my face as I grabbed my crotch. I fainted right in front of him. The medic got down with me. He shook me. I was slow to respond. The medic asked me, "What unit are you with? Are you all right?"

"I feel weak, Doc. I'm with Echo Company, Second Battalion, Fifth Cavalry Division. The medic then said, "Where are you coming from, soldier?"

"I'm coming back from R & R in Singapore."

"The sergeant in charge has to know what's going on." The medic managed to help me get up. We found a folding chair not far away. My focus was blurred. The inside of the tent was dark. It was set up almost like a hospital, with all the medical instruments and supplies lying around on tables. I saw a few wounded soldiers who had just come from out of the field, lying on gurneys, getting treated. Soon the medic came back with a captain. The captain told me, "I want you to get up and pull down your pants so we can see what's going on." I got up and pulled down my fatigues pants as the discharge became more pronounced. The captain then said, "How long have you been on R & R?"

"I was on R & R for a week."

"Son, you got syphilis. You'll have to stay back here in the rear until this clears up."

My heart sank. I didn't know how serious this was or how long I would be back in the rear. The captain said, "We'll have to get you assigned to a unit while you're here so this can clear up. So what we have to do now is get this procedure started so you can get back to your fighting strength. You'll have to get two penicillin shots for the next five days." The medic brought over the syringes to get started. The syringe was full of penicillin.

My back was turned from the medic as I bent down to take the medicine. I grimaced as a needle went in each buttock. The other medics went about their business of treating the wounded. The sweat dripped from me as I pulled my pants up. "Will I get a purple heart for this captain?" The captain looked at me and said, "Just be here tomorrow at about the same time." Two shots in the buttocks wasn't any pleasure because it was just as hard as having this thing called syphilis. I was able to observe what was going on back in the rear encampment. It was a much different duty than being out in the field.

The base itself was well armed as troops would come and go after being out in the field. There were some soldiers who were permanently assigned to the rear area. These soldiers were clerks, cooks, engineers, and medics, along with other essential personnel who would back up the troops out in the field. The troops in the rear would sometimes have their own Vietnamese maids who would come in and do various duties for the soldiers that were stationed there. Their sleeping quarters were much different than the hooches out in the field. Even though the rear was a little secure than out in the field, you were still in Vietnam, subject to attack at any time. I was assigned to guard duty on the perimeter at the large bunkers. Nights spent on guard duty at the bunkers would remind me of what was happening out in the field. I would see gunships making contact about twenty miles out or so, spraying their ammunition from the guns of the ships. The light show was still very much live. The tracers and return fire were being engaged, which reminded me that soon I would be back out there in the action. My gun position would be right next to the .50-caliber machine gun on the perch of the bunker that I was assigned to.

My strength started to come back as the penicillin shots started to take effect. There was one instance when I was on my way to chow when I saw some black soldiers congregating together near a fortified hooch, who were smoking grass from a pipe. The soldiers looked like they might belong to a line company that was out in the field. Some of them could have been stationed right there at Bien Hoa. I passed by the one soldier that was smoking on the pipe. He said, "Hey, black brother, we got a pipe over here we been hitting on. You want some of this weed to take your mind off this fucking place! You are a brother, aren't you?" I hesitated as I turned and saw the soldier extend the pipe to me.

The soldier tempted me to the offer until I noticed a jeep with two MPs approaching us from the back of the soldier with the pipe. The white and the black soldier were out on patrol. One of the soldiers turned around to see what I was looking at. The soldier then said, Hey! The MPs are coming! We'd better get out of here!" The soldier holding the pipe laid it under a steel pot that was on the ground as if nothing was going on. The group of black soldiers started to scatter out in various directions. The short-lived life in the rear had come to an end after the succession of shots for syphilis.

At LZ Ike, the insurgency was still going on around the perimeter. I learned that a small platoon of Echo Company had been ambushed twice outside the perimeter. There was one instance when the patrol was ambushed by giant bees as the patrol ran into a huge nest. The bees attacked as if they were Vietcong. The soldiers made their presence known when they radioed into the perimeter about what was happening.

They told headquarters to announce a cease-fire so that they wouldn't be in the midst of gun fire coming from the LZ. The announcement was made. "Cease fire! Cease fire! Cease fire! We got a patrol coming back in!" Everybody on the perimeter heard the screams of the soldiers who made their appearance as they ran from the wood line, swatting at large bees. They ran back into the perimeter as if they had seen a ghost.

There were a few of the soldiers who were so scared that they left their M.16s near the trail where they had been attacked by the bees. The medics immediately attended to these soldiers who were in shock. I saw the big welts that had been inflicted from the stingers on the soldier's faces and hands and in the tops of their heads.

There was another incident that happened while just being back at the LZ. A patrol went out to do some more reconnaissance, which were about eight men on this particular day. It happened about midday as I saw them go out in the field from my mortar pit. Included in this patrol was Carlos, who carried the .60 machine gun. As they went out, the sergeant said to them as they were leaving the perimeter, "We're not going to be out for too long, so remember that we're out here!" I looked back at Sergeant Greely as he acknowledged what the sergeant said. It wasn't long before gunfire was heard, and Sergeant Greely announced, "All right, troops, we got a patrol in trouble out there, so cease fire until you hear further from me!" While wiping down the .81-millimeter mortar, the commotion came into existence.

The communication was heard on the radio along with gun fire. The sergeant on the radio said, "Get down, men! All right, Carlos, I want you to give those troops some cover!" The firefight seemed like it had gotten intense as I said to my new squad, "All right, get your steel pots and flight vest on just in case we get hit!" Soon the patrol emerged from the wood line. The troops moved low in a crouched position, trying to duck the onslaught of attackers. Carlos backed up from the rear as he fired the .60 machine gun nonstop.

The cease-fire was still in effect as all the soldiers made it back inside the perimeter. The troops seemed exhausted and acted as if their fate of staying alive was still with them. The insurgency of enemy that had confronted them was starting to receive fire from helicopters that had been dispatched. They swarmed the area where the soldiers had just come from. The soldiers were breathing hard as they came in from the helicopter pad, being followed by mortar rounds from the enemy. My mortar squad returned fire with ferociousness. The insurgency of Vietnamese soldiers retreated because of the onslaught of counter fire. Then there came a lull.

The troops were exhausted as they made their presence inside the perimeter. They began to drink from their canteens. It wasn't long after when Sergeant Greely emerged and greeted the troops. He said, "I heard you all ran into Charlie. I've been told that Carlos saved your asses." Carlos sat next to the mortar pit, inspecting his machine gun. He wanted to make sure it would continue to be in good working order. Sergeant Greely came over to him and said, "Carlos, you're going to be put in for the Silver Star for what you did out there. So don't get cocky because you deserve it, amigo. I want you guys to thank your lucky stars that no one got hurt!"

The event had given Echo Company a little relief that this particular patrol had once again made it back safe. I was starting to adjust to my new squad. It was only three of us, so it would be on-the-job training for the new men. This was a squad that I wanted to see under fire because now these were black troops who would have to show their prowess. Specialist Smith was on rotation from Germany. He was about my height. He had been stuck back in the rear for a little while doing guard duty. So this LZ experience would be much different for him than being back in the rear. His stature was he wanted to be a good field soldier, which he was now because it was a position he accepted.

So it was like he would get more of a taste of combat by being out in the field with the enemy. I felt good about Smith because he just looked like he could fight. At least his experience back in the rear gave him some idea of what incoming was like. Smith was very dark or what you might say looked like blue black. He had close-cropped hair and even small squinted eyes, which made you think he might have had some Oriental in him.

He was of good character at this point because the real impact of combat had not hit him yet. He did what was expected in the squad in order for him to help make it run. He had that down-home work ethic that was from the fields of South Carolina. When I first met Smith, I could tell that he had been in the country for a little while. I could tell he had been in the rear because his boots weren't that broken in.

The first day when I and Specialist Smith met was when I was coming from the ordeal at Bien Hoa. Sergeant Greely was waiting for us when we got off the helicopter arriving at LZ Ike. Sergeant Greely told me that Smith would be in my squad. Sergeant Greely knew that having good men in your squad was important.

I began to work on the remnants of my new mortar pit that was somewhat still in disarray while being away. The fact that Sergeant Greely had told me that I was getting new men made me ready to receive them. In the process of all this happening, I would see Ishmal, Jason, and Scott passing by the mortar pit. My guess was that they were members of another squad now. Awareness came over me when they were around. Sergeant Greely also saw them going toward the helicopter pad. Sergeant Greely said, "Durham, this is the new man who'll be working with you. He's been doing a lot of guard duty back in the rear. Put him to work so we can get this mortar pit up and running. You know what to do, so show this man the ropes."

I said, "You can put your gear in the hooch because we got some sand bags to get filled." Smith's response was quick as he discarded some of his gear, with the exception of his M.16. "I see you have a flight vest and steel pot because you're going to need them while you're out here. So keep them close by, we also have to get some more ammo.

"I'll show you how to break open boxes and how to get the ammo ready. We have to hurry up because you never know when Charlie is going to hit us." Specialist Smith went to work right away as he listened very carefully to what I was saying. Then Sergeant Greely said, "Durham, you'll have another man who will come join you at about 0200. We're still low on man power, so this is all we can spare right now."

"Okay, Sarge, every little bit helps."

Soon the other new man would come to my squad. He was a transfer from a line company. When he arrived, he was kind of small and scruffy looking, with a narrow head and small features. It seemed almost like his fatigues were falling off him. It still didn't stop him from being weighted down with all the necessary combat gear that was needed. I could tell that he was a fighting soldier. His appearance just gave me the impression that he wanted to live. Just by the way his fatigues were dirty from the jungle. The mortar pit position would be a little relief for him. The men listened with intent to the conversation that was about to take place. Sergeant Greely introduced the new soldier. "Durham, this is the other man that I said I'd get you, so go ahead and break him in. I have to get back to headquarters. There's been a lot of movement up north, so I'll have to talk to you all later."

Greely went back to headquarters. The new man looked at my stripes on my shoulders. The soldier appeared to me as if he were about to starve. I looked at the soldier and said, "My name is Sergeant Durham. Are you hungry? Where is your steel pot and flight vest?" The soldier pulled off his ruck sack and began to go through it. With his additional gear, he managed to pull out his steel pot and flight vest. I said, "What is your name?"

The soldier then said, "My name is Johnson, and I've just come from out of the boonies. I'm from Chicago, and I have five children. So that's why I'm here so that I can feed my family. I didn't want to come to Vietnam but got drafted. My sergeant decided to send me to a reconnaissance company. So here I am." I said, "You thought you were going to get out of the field." We both laughed for a brief moment. We looked over at Smith who was filling sand bags.

The soldier then asked, "Where can I put the rest of my equipment? He held on to his M.16."

"We only have a small hooch, so you can put some of your equipment in the hooch and keep you're 16 out in the pit. I looked down into his ruck sack. Specialist Johnson had an assortment of grenades in his ruck sack. "You can get rid of those grenades, we don't have any use for them in the pit. You can give them to one of those guys in the line companies who will need them more than you do. We don't want one of them things to bounce back near us." I began to build trust in Johnson and Smith. This was something that had to happen right away because we would be fighting next to one another. I had to know where they were coming from because time had gotten short. There still was no room for mistakes.

Johnson and Smith went about their duties as if this mortar squad was somewhere they wanted to be. These men seemed to me to be men that I could trust. I gave the men their guard assignments as evening came. I told the men as the sun went down, "We are in for another rude awakening," as they ate from their c rations. "Stay on your toes." They looked at each other in disappointment. The only thing we have to do is be ready. The mess tent was about two hundred yards from the mortar pit. It could serve most of the men on the LZ. This was a new mess tent, which was as big as a small house. The dark green canopy made it stand out. The cooks still had M.16s in case they needed to go to a bunker for support.

The men's four-hour shifts seemed to be in working order. I took the last shift right before sun rise. It was right after midnight. The men suffered from insomnia. Everybody seemed as if they wanted to be up until daylight. They would get up out of the hooch and walk around it from time to time. It was not too long after they had been up for a little while when I noticed some soldiers walking past the mortar pit. It was Ishmal, Jason, and Scott. I confronted them. "Where are you all going this time of night?" Ishmal answered with arrogance in his voice. "Oh, what's it to you? We're just going down to the mess tent to get something to eat." The other two soldiers, Scott and Jason, backed him by saying, "It's none of your business where we're going. We're not in your squad anymore, so don't worry about it."

"I still out rank you and can give you an order." I noticed none of them had their helmets or flight vests on. "You all need your flight vests and helmets on."

They looked at me and gave me no response. They were soon inside the dark mess tent. It was not long after that incoming rockets, mortars, RPGs, and AK-47s opened up and started making their way from out of the wood lines to inside of the perimeter. My squad was a quick response. The squad responded as the mortar was being fed. Johnson and Smith got in their proper positions, handling the adrenaline rush, which they weren't going to let consume them. Their energy was heightened as they got the proper charges off and passed the mortar rounds to me, who was positioned at the mortar.

My speed of getting the rounds out was unparalleled as they were delivered into the wood line. I hastened my squad on with the amount of relentlessness that I had gotten accustomed to. At the same time, the enemies' rounds impacted all around the mortar pit. Shrapnel pierced the sand bags and kicked up dirt as I heard small pieces of shrapnel hit against the mortar. The idea was to disregard the rounds' impact inside the perimeter. It was important to make sure you countered enemy fire even more ferociously than the enemy.

The counter fire was quick and steady as rounds were sent out. I traversed and maneuvered the mortar to its proper targets. Some enemy rounds made direct hits on the inside of the perimeter. Several rockets found their way to the mess tent where Jason, Ishmal, and Scott had just entered. They were defenseless. This attack kept up a good pace as Joe and the bunker personnel kept busy as claymores and grenade launchers were being initiated. Some of the enemy cut their way through the razor wire to get inside the perimeter.

Joe shot down several enemy soldiers as he used the .50-caliber machine gun with intensity. An enemy was shot by Johnson as he stood up inside the perimeter just past Joe. The .60 machine guns opened up on both sides of Joe's bunker. There was one .60 machine gunner to the left of Joe who killed several enemy soldiers who tried to breach the perimeter.

There was another enemy soldier who penetrated the other bunker to the far left, igniting himself with a satchel charge that blew him up. One Vietnamese soldier had also made it inside the perimeter, which had both of his arms blown off, perhaps by the .60 or the .50. He soon dropped once he had made it inside. He fell right outside of the mortar pit. Soon the appearance of the gunships were making their presence known as the fighting continued. They had been notified of the positions of the enemy beyond the wood lines. This was near the area where the artillery was doing their business. The mortar squad did not miss a beat as everybody in the squad was in sync. Everyone in the squad was shaken but stepped up to the task at hand. It was a controlled nervousness that had to be monitored. Smith and Johnson were shaken but fought along with me as if their lives depended on it.

The medics with their stretchers were starting to make their presence as a lull in the fighting took place. The medics were able to go about their duties. I looked down where the mess tent was and saw by the illumination of flares that Ishmal, Jason, and Scott had emerged. They were the walking wounded. All three were walking toward the mortar pit with the help of medics so that they could be led out to where the helicopters were landing. I saw that Scott had blistering shrapnel wounds, which were on his back; Jason's fingers on his right hand were dangling and barely staying on. The gaping wound was evident as I saw Ishmal with a patch of skin that was taken out the back of his head. His skull was exposed. He was in shock. They gazed over at me as they passed by the mortar pit. Our eyes met as if to say, "We wished we had listened to you about having the necessary equipment on."

At this point, it was too late. The damage had been done. Morning had finally arrived. The aftermath of the battle was made evident. The disarray of LZ Ike was present again as the bodies were being policed up by troops who were assigned to that duty. All my squad did was watch and prepare the mortar pit for the next attack. They continued with their jobs to shore up the mortar pit. There was a black trooper named Mike. He would act as a utility man, driving the mule around the perimeter for various tasks. His job was also to transport equipment around the perimeter. He would also traverse the perimeter, looking for filled body bags. Mike looked over at the side of the mortar pit where a Vietnamese soldier had been mortally wounded. This was the soldier that had lost both his arms. He was barely breathing. Mike drove the mule up near the mortar pit. Mike was kind of burly, with sloppy hanging fatigues on his body. He got off the mule to look at and inspect the almost dying soldier. It was only a matter of time when the soldier would be dead. Mike jumped off the jeep and stood over the soldier in a menacing manner. The soldier was heaving for air as he lay on the ground naked, with his clothes torn off. Mike unbuttoned his fatigue pants and pulled out his penis. He began peeing on the dying soldier. I jumped over the pit and pushed Mike away from the soldier and said, "Don't do that, Mike! Can't you see the man is getting ready to die!" Mike's response was, "Fuck that stupid son of a bitch! He deserved what he got!"

That day had passed, and it almost seemed like everything was getting back in order. I took my turn in line while waiting for chow. There must have been about twenty troops in line waiting for a hot meal when Carlos cut line while pushing me to the side. He pulled me back as he got in the front. My reaction was immediate. I thought what had just happened was rude. I shoved back at Carlos, but it seemed as if Carlos wanted to take it a little further. A scuffle took place. Carlos wanted to manhandle me. The incident had gone too far. We started to wrestle. The first thing that came to my mind was the fact that I had to body slam Carlos. I got up under him and slammed him to the ground. It did not matter to me that he had just gotten the Silver Star. I was on top of Carlos, looking down at him. The match was won by me. While on top, I asked Carlos,

"What are you trying to prove, Carlos! You should know that you can't beat me! You're just too light in the ass!" There was soon a tap on my shoulder. I looked up and saw that it was a lieutenant colonel. The colonel said, "All right, son, break it up before you both get into trouble."

Carlos and I decided to get up as if nothing had happened. The camaraderie between me Johnson and Smith was beginning to take shape as we went about the business of operating like a mortar squad. Johnson would talk about his family in Chicago. Smith was more or less the free spirit. I and Smith seemed to really relate to each other. He would tell me about his good times in Germany before he came to Vietnam. We would take pictures of each other to send back to South Carolina.

The time to get back to the States was getting closer and closer. This was the period of enhanced anxiety because there seemed to be a high amount of rotation. New troops still rotated to the unit. Antiwar protesters were doing their thing back in the states in which we knew nothing about. They weren't regular troops but were coming from the National Guard. All I knew was that the enemy was still on the attack. I wanted to keep my morale up because I was getting close to going home. There was nothing now that was going to distract me from completing this mission. A new lieutenant had just arrived from the National Guard. His name was Lieutenant Greaves. He was slender, almost geek looking in appearance. He had the textbook appearance of an officer to go along with his stature. When this lieutenant appeared, he seemed as if he were some kind of inspector. He would be a part of my squad until it was time for me to depart. I had learned not to let anyone come to my squad expecting to take over. The same principle would apply to this officer that I knew nothing about. There was mistrust for the National Guard and the Reservists who were mostly back in the states. It had been felt that these volunteers were trying to get out of being in combat.

Lieutenant Greaves took an opposite view. I had to watch him closely. Having someone watch over you with only a few more weeks to go in the country made me feel uneasy to say the least. It made me even more uneasy because the lieutenant had not been in the country that long. I managed to get some crayons and have a picture of an elephant on paper. This drawing had thirty days of blocks in squares. I colored the days that went by while in my hooch. I would keep the elephant calendar in a safe place in my ruck sack. The elephant calendar was halfway colored at this point in my tour.

I started coloring the elephant from the top down. Now I was at a point where I was halfway down the elephant. This would add to the intrigue of knowing that maybe I was going to make it. I didn't want to get overly confident, so some reserve had to be shown as a veteran soldier. Soon I was back in the mortar pit. I asked Smith, "What is it like in Germany?" Smith sat over in the corner of the mortar pit, shaving off a piece of bark that he had found. The military knife he had was glistening from the moonlight that was available. Smith had on his helmet and flight vest, which covered his black torso.

Smith answered, "Man, it was nice in Germany. I kind of wish I was there, but they sent me over to this hellhole! I liked the German women. We called them *Fräulein*. They would treat you real good! They liked the black GIs. They were just a whole lot different than the women back in the States. They were not prejudiced!" I then said, "Man, I wouldn't mind going there, but all I want to do now is get back to the states. I'm so short, I feel like I'm about an inch off the ground. Pretty soon, you won't be able to see me. I'll be so short." Smith looked over at Carroll and smiled. We both laughed for that brief moment.

It was then that the whistling sounds of the incoming rounds started making their way in from the outside of the perimeter. It was almost like it was a drill, but this was the real deal. It was something I would never get used to. Smith scrambled and got in low crawl position to start getting rounds ready for me. I yelled out, "Incoming! Incoming! Incoming!" The incoming rounds made their way inside the perimeter. The peace had been broken. Johnson and the new lieutenant emerged from the hooch. I could see the flashes in the wood line where the rounds were coming from. The outgoing .81-millimeter rounds made their way to the wood line. We had already put out about ten rounds. The lieutenant colonel was hunched down as he watched the flashes that were taking place inside the wood line with his binoculars.

The lieutenant colonel then said, "Let me help you!" I stood away from the mortar tube for a moment. He said, "I want you to go out and line up those stakes or send one of your men out to line them up so we can hit those targets!" We looked at the lieutenant colonel like he was crazy. The lieutenant colonel attempted to adjust the mortar while looking through the sight. I reacted right away. I stepped over to where the lieutenant was trying to direct the mortar. The lieutenant didn't realize that he was taking up precious time that we couldn't afford to be wasted. There had to be counter fire while incoming was impacting around us. I took it upon myself to push the lieutenant to the side and said, "We don't have time to go and put up any stakes! They're on top of us! We need to get these rounds out!" I proceeded with the help of the men to feed the mortar and hit the targets without the use of the stakes because of my experience. One of the candy-cane poles was hit by a rocket. This didn't mean that the mortar was not fixed on its target. It was a matter of speed, which the rest of my crew knew how to handle.

It was soon afterward that the lieutenant realized that going out and messing with the stakes would have been a foolish mistake. Incoming rounds were raining inside the razor wire near where the stakes were positioned. My reaction and that of my crew was the right move because the incoming rounds had to be countered. The fighting would continue with no let up as the lieutenant decided to be an armed guard inside the mortar pit, looking out with his M.16. I and my mortar crew continued to perform as I walked the rounds along the wood line.

I would make the rounds zigzag to confuse the enemy. I made a cross to cover the area where the enemy was. The enemy was all confused. The idea of not letting up was in my consciousness. I just knew the right amount of charges to take off the mortar as I traversed and winded the mortar up to track down the enemy. My directions to Smith and Johnson were to keep Charlie off us. There was no pause as sweat seeped through the fatigues and streamed down our bodies with all our little bit of armor on.

In the midst of LZ Ike just before sunset, a line of 12 soldiers stood at attention. Their fatigues were partially cleaned as they looked straight ahead. General Abrams stood in front of Carlos, with an officer next to him, who had a cushion of medals in his hand who stood next to me. The General had just finished pinning the Silver Star on him. The general moved in front of me as I saluted. As he pinned the Bronze Star on me, he said, "It is rare that a soldier would get three Bronze Stars." "Job well done. You are an asset to your country." We both saluted one another.

It was told to me by a messenger in the following days that I would be going to the rear. This was where I was going to leave from going back to the states. Bien Hoa was my next destination. My gear was packed and ready to go. On this afternoon, there was a sigh of relief. Just remembering what it would be like for me to go home gave me a sense of worth, knowing that my job in Vietnam was just about over. Before the incident with the lieutenant, I was reminded of my hometown. There was a line company that had come in from out of the field. It was the dusty look of a line company coming in that got my attention. They were coming in from the field for a stand-down. The worn-out soldiers seemed tired. The boonies had given the soldiers the worn-out look.

The next thing I heard was my name being called. "Carroll! Carroll! Carroll! Carroll." I looked down at the line of soldiers making their way inside the perimeter. I almost didn't recognize the Southern voice. It was Jimmy, the white boy from Sumter. I shaded over my eyes to make sure it was Jimmy. I then said, "Jimmy! Jimmy! Is that you?" By the look of Jimmy, he had become a hardened-looking soldier. It was like he wasn't the same boy that I had met at the recruiting station back in Sumter.

Jimmy had turned into a true grunt. Jimmy was dressed with the dirt and agony of the jungle life for an American soldier in Vietnam. We ran to each other and embraced. Jimmy said, "I'm glad to see you, Carroll! Look, we're both still alive and in one piece!" I laughed and said, "Yeah, man, and we're both getting short! Soon we'll be back in Sumter!" The greeting lasted briefly because Jimmy had to join back with his company. I would never see Jimmy again.

All the necessary gear that I had now was all I wanted to take back to the rear. I walked into headquarters where Captain Wright was waiting. He was consulting with his subordinates. He turned and looked at me. He responded, "I heard you're getting ready to leave, Durham?"

"Yeah, Captain. I think this is just about it." Captain Wright extended his arm for a handshake. It was mutual as Captain Wright told me, "You've done a good job, Durham, so now we are going to see if we can get you out of here."

"I'm ready to go home, Captain."

The arrival in the rear area was uneventful as I checked into the outprocessing center. I was directed to a building where I would be staying for little while in Bien Hoa. It was a small building on the style of a barracks, which the engineers had constructed. My old fatigues were replaced with a new pair, which I had received with the rest of the clothes that I had stored. My M.16 had been turned in to the armory. While getting all this done, Bien Hoa was still getting hit by mortars.

It was sporadic but still enough to let me know that I still might not get out of Vietnam in one piece. My meals were eaten in a large cafeteria that looked like an airplane hangar. There must have been a hundred troops there getting ready to go home. My time had gotten down to a couple of days. The barrack that I stayed in looked like a small house. I wondered if I could tolerate being uncomfortable on this level, knowing that Bien Hoa was well fortified.

In the small bungalow-type barrack, there were about two men in two different bunks of which two were empty. I chose a bottom bunk while noticing the bunk above mine was occupied with a soldier that looked like he was writing a letter. This would be my last sleeping quarters in Vietnam. At this time, I had very little to say to the soldier that was inside the dwelling. I did notice that the soldier had a Big Red One patch on his shoulder. On this evening before departure, the soldier in the upper bunk above started talking to me.

He looked down into my bunk as I looked at my short-time calendar. He said, "Hey, soldier, my name is Steve." "Looks like you're getting pretty short by the way that elephant looks!" I replied as I looked up and smiled at the somewhat handsome soldier who was lying there in his bunk. I looked up at him and smiled. "Yeah, that's right, you might say that." Then the soldier replied, "Hey! Do you want to go down to a bar tonight? There's a little bar down the road that I checked out last night. It seemed like it was all right. Let's go down and have a few drinks to get our mind off this fucking place for a little while. My plane is leaving early in the morning, and I plan to be on it. How about that, homeboy! We getting ready to go back to the world!"

Without hesitation I said, "Okay, my name is Durham, and you ain't said nothing but a word! I could use a couple of drinks because my bird is leaving tomorrow evening!" We both made our way down to the bar that evening. The bar wasn't that big as we entered the cabin-type building. It seemed to accommodate a small amount of soldiers that were passing through. The atmosphere was dark as there were dimly lit lamps, which were scattered around and hanging from the ceiling. There were a few lamps that lit the area of the bar where the drinks were located. There also was the sound of a generator running outside the facility.

There were about twelve stools at the bar as we approached it. There was some activity going on with other military personnel who were mingling with other soldiers who were drinking and talking. I noticed a cute little Vietnamese barmaid, who was serving drinks. There was a middle-aged Vietnamese woman who was working the cash register. I called to the woman working the cash register and said, "Excuse me, miss, can a GI get a drink around here?" She shut the register and looked my way. She then said, "What kind of drink do you want, GI?"

"Give me a scotch and ginger ale!" I pointed to an empty table not too far from the bar where I and Steve would be sitting. "I'll be sitting at the table over there." I nudged Steve and pointed to the table once again. "Come on, Steve, get your drink and let's sit at that table over there."

Steve ordered his drink. We both went to the table that I pointed out. The bar room had started to grow louder as more troops started entering the bar. The pretty little Vietnamese barmaid approached the table with the drinks that we had ordered. I noticed that Steve had gotten the attention of another barmaid. We both devoured the couple of drinks that we had. The glasses were empty. We devoured several more drinks. Suddenly, I began to feel the effects of the drinks. I got more intrigued with the barmaid who had caught my attention. She had managed to give me a flashback of Leea that I had fallen in love with out in the field. I called the girl over from the bar because she continued to give me the eye. She approached me. I said, "Have a seat. I need to talk to you." I then said, "You understand English, don't you?"

The girl looked at me and smiled; she said, "I speak *tee tee* English."

"Oh, you mean you speak a little bit of English. I'm getting ready to go back to America! My plane leaves tomorrow. You are very beautiful. You are number 1. I need a wife. Do you know what I mean?" She looked at me and nodded her head up and down in excitement. I don't want to go back to America by myself. You can come with me so we can get married! I gently put my hand on the right side of the woman's cheek. I gazed into her eyes and grabbed her hand. "You listen to me. We can go and get married tomorrow!"

The Vietnamese girl was all smiles as she forgot the fact that she was a barmaid. I had mesmerized her at this point. She was interested in hearing more. "Tomorrow I'll come get you, and we can go to headquarters to get the paperwork we need. We'll have to go to see the chaplain." I lifted the girl's hand and gave it a gentle kiss. "You meet me here tomorrow." She shook her head in delight. "I need to go get some sleep, so I'll be back tomorrow to get you!"

I looked at Steve and said, "I'll see you in the morning, man." I had a steady walk out of the bar. As soon as I left the club, a fight ensued between two soldiers from different units. My cautious journey back to the barrack was uneventful as I staggered up to the door. The next morning, in a slight haze I realized this was the day of my departure from Vietnam. Steve was already up, putting his gear into his duffel bag. By being awoken in a stupor with my clothes on amazed me. The look at Steve was blurred. "It was kind of wild down at that club last night. I told this girl that I was going to marry her and bring her back to the States." Steve said, "Oh yeah! You're right, it did get kind of wild down there last night." Then Steve said, "Yeah, and another thing, I heard at breakfast that a GI got his throat cut by one of those girls down at the bar."

"What! Are you serious!" Steve then said, "I'm serious as a heart attack."

Steve picked up his gear. He was all packed. He said as he stepped out the door, "I'll see you back in the world, brother." We both embraced. He then walked out the door. I knew that my turn would be next. I day dreamed what I told the girl at the bar while packing my gear. I decided that I wasn't going back to the bar that I was at the previous night. The image came in my mind that the woman I told that I was going to marry cut the GI's throat. I walked out of the barrack and looked in the direction of the bar. I walked in the opposite direction. While in the cafeteria, I knew this was going to be my last meal.

The line was long as I stood waiting with about one hundred soldiers ready to go home. I noticed a group of black soldiers who were standing around together. They were giving one another the dap (a series of handshake greetings for black soldiers) while standing in the chow line. I did not know all the sequences of the dap. I could do the basic dap. There was one menacing-looking slim dark-skinned soldier who seemed to be the center of attention as he was displaying his very good skill of doing the dap.

He could do the modified black handshake in about twenty or so sequences. I watched the hand slaps and grips in rhythmic motion. I felt intimidated because of my basic skill. The black soldier who was doing the dap approached me while I was in line. He gave me the fist to get the sequence started. I made an attempt and managed to get out of sequence to my slight embarrassment. The soldier then gave me the most unusual stare. I told the soldier, "Man, I've been out in the field. I wasn't exactly concentrating on learning how to do the dap." The soldier gave me another stare and walked off.

The chow line was slowly led up to the feeding area. Soon the thumping sounds of mortars started hitting around the outside of the cafeteria. *Thump! Thump! Thump! Thump!* The sound still put chills through my spine as everyone got under the cafeteria tables as the last defense. The movements of the veterans made them react at the same time. I got through my meal after, still wondering whether or not I would get out of Vietnam alive. I gathered up my gear for the final time. I looked at myself in the narrow mirror that was in the bungalow. Along the way, I decided to stop by the post exchange to buy a fifth of Wild Turkey whiskey. After buying the whiskey, I loaded it into my duffel bag. The airstrip where my departure was going to take place looked the same as when I first got to Vietnam. While sitting under a canopy on a picnic table, I decided to pull the big bottle out of my bag as I looked at the assortment of military planes. I gazed at the bottle and got a flashback of the time when I first got in the country. I proceeded to open the bottle and lifted it up to my lips. The whiskey poured down my throat as if it was coming from a faucet. My plane had just approached as the stairs were being put in front of the door. I put the bottle down as I turned to the side and saw a pallet of .81-millimeter mortar rounds peeking out from the five-feet-tall pallet stack. I would not take the bottle on the plane. It was half-full as I laid it on top of the pallet.

It was the Fourth of July in 1979 when I sat on the redline. I was dressed in a business suit while a little boy played with a GI Joe doll. The doll slipped out of his hand and ended up in front of my seat. I picked up the GI Joe doll and smiled at it.

The end

THE WHITE HOUSE

May 21, 2010

Mr. Carroll A. Durham, Jr.
1026 Elm Ridge Avenue
Baltimore, Maryland 21229-5323

Dear Carroll:

I am pleased to write on behalf of my mother, who very much appreciated your thoughtful comments.

We are blessed that my mother was able to come with us to the White House. It has made the transition from our home in Chicago so much easier for our family, especially our daughters. We all have settled quite smoothly into our new surroundings and routines, and my mother has been a steady hand throughout that process.

But even with many changes for our family, it's also clear that we are at a unique moment in our country's history. And so, in the spirit of the many generations of Americans whose labor and service made our Nation great, I encourage you to find new ways to strengthen America by serving your community. I want to thank you for the work you're already doing, and know that your continued engagement is vital as we move forward together.

Thanks again for writing. I wish all the best for you and those close to you.

Sincerely,

Michelle Obama

Edwards Brothers Malloy
Thorofare, NJ USA
March 13, 2014